Thinking to Transform

Reflection in Leadership Learning

A Volume in
Contemporary Perspectives on Leadership Learning

Series Editor:
Kathie L. Guthrie, *Florida State University*

Contemporary Perspectives on Leadership Learning

Kathie L. Guthrie, Series Editor

Thinking to Transform

Reflection in Leadership Learning

By

Jillian M. Volpe White and Kathy L. Guthrie
Florida State University

and

Maritza Torres
University of Central Florida

Information Age Publishing, Inc.
Charlotte, North Carolina • www.infoagepub.com

Library of Congress Cataloging-in-Publication Data

CIP data for this book can be found on the Library of Congress website:
http://www.loc.gov/index.html

Paperback: 978-1-64113-821-5
Hardcover: 978-1-64113-822-2
E-Book: 978-1-64113-823-9

Printed in the United States of America.

*For the people who are our support structures
for reflection in leadership learning.*

CONTENTS

ACKNOWLEDGMENTS

It is both beautiful and challenging to organize significant but nebulous concepts, like reflection and leadership, into a cohesive text. The process of writing this book has necessarily been reflective, resulting in our own aha moments and perspective changes. As a team of authors, it has been fascinating to consider how our individual perspectives, informed by our identities and experiences, shaped our collective understanding of reflection in leadership learning.

This book was supported by a community of reflective practitioners. We are grateful for Brittany Devies who read the first drafts and asked questions which caused us to pause, reflect, and rewrite. We are also grateful to Daniel Marshall and Kaitlin Wallace who provided challenging and supportive feedback; we are particularly appreciative of all the times you both read "just one more paragraph." As brilliant and reflective individuals, we are excited for what all of you bring to this work. We are in awe of how Sally Watkins took the images we dreamed about and sketched on scraps of paper and brought them to life.

Adding to the body of scholarly work is a privilege that requires an investment of time and energy; this sometimes means taking time to read, write, or think instead of something else that is equally important. We are grateful to the partners, family, friends, and colleagues who provided support and created space for us to read, write, and reflect.

CHAPTER 1

INTO THE WOODS

Setting Up Significance

Images are powerful tools for remembering and thinking about experiences. Images may jog our memories or elicit emotions. Envision for a moment an image of a bay at sunset. In the foreground, there is a small tree which is backlit by a pale blue sky dotted with wispy clouds in shades of light pink and deep purple. In the middle of the bay is a sailboat. The water is so smooth you can see a clear reflection of the sky in the water. This image resonates with reflection in three ways. First, there is literal reflection; the water is so smooth, you can see the sky reflected on the glassy surface. In some ways, reflection in leadership learning is like holding up a mirror to ourselves and our experiences to ask "Who am I?" and "Who do I want to become?" Second, when the person who took the photo looks at it, they might think back to their experience. Who were they with? How did they feel? What was their experience? How are they different now than they were then? And finally, if a group of people were all in this same place at the same time and they each took a picture of the same thing, the images would be similar but not exactly alike. By putting the images together, you would have a better sense of the whole experience than you would with any single image. This speaks to the power of collective reflection and shared experiences for learning.

Now imagine a salient experience in your leadership learning process. What image stands out from that experience? Where were you? With

Thinking to Transform: Reflection in Leadership Learning
pp. 1–23
Copyright © 2019 by Information Age Publishing

whom did you share this experience? What made this experience stand out? What did you learn from this experience? How are you different now than you were in that moment? How did this experience empower and enable you to create change? In this book, we focus on the theory and practice of reflection in leadership learning as a catalyst for individual, group, and community growth that facilitates positive change.

THE REASON FOR THIS BOOK

Reflection is an essential element of the learning process, and an integral component of leadership learning. Leadership development is an important aim of education. Leadership learning is an active and experiential process (Guthrie & Jenkins, 2018). However, it is not experience that is educative, but the reflection following an experience that results in the greatest benefit (Ash & Clayton, 2009). Through reflection people make meaning of experiences and reconsider their actions and beliefs. It is incumbent upon experiential leadership educators to incorporate reflection into experiences. As the field of leadership learning expands in both breadth and depth, understanding how reflection underscores leadership can help practitioners and faculty members shape curricular and cocurricular programming to enhance students' leadership learning.

This book calls attention to the importance of prioritizing time to think with intentionality, both individually and in community. Reflection is key for identity development and authentic self-understanding; this facilitates relationship building for strong teams and groups which supports the leadership process. Turkle (2015) described a cycle whereby,

> solitude reinforces a secure sense of self, and with that, the capacity for empathy. Then, conversation with others provides rich material for self-reflection. Just as alone we prepare to talk together, together we learn how to engage in a more productive solitude. (p. 10)

Indeed, with an increasing reliance on technology to escape feelings of boredom (Turkle, 2015) and greater time spent with people who are similar to us (Bahns, Preacher, Crandall, & Gillath, 2016), the capacity for self-evaluation and critical examination of beliefs may be in jeopardy. Reflection allows learners to meaningfully evaluate their beliefs and actions. This is essential for leadership learning as students explore their identity and capacity to develop leadership self-efficacy (Bertrand Jones, Guthrie, & Osteen, 2016). Through examining their assumptions and beliefs in the context of social and political contexts, students may engage in critical reflection and take action for justice. At a time in history with numerous multifaceted challenges, reflection is critical for leadership learning.

Reflection creates a bridge between thoughts and actions. It is a skill and a process which allows people to learn and apply new knowledge. Reflection includes both the cognitive process of making meaning and the methods used by learners to describe what happened, draw connections between experiences, synthesize learning, and develop insights for future application (Kolb, 1984). We explore reflection as a philosophy; a component of experiential leadership learning; an instructional strategy and tool for learning assessment; a form of and complement to contemplative practice; and the methods which facilitate the aforementioned functions. There are a myriad of definitions for reflection, and in Chapter 2, we explore reflection in greater depth.

It is important to distinguish between leader (the person) and leadership (the process) (Dugan & Komives, 2011); using the terms interchangeably can lead to confusion, undermine postindustrial models of leadership, and prevent educators from engaging all students in the leadership process (Guthrie & Jenkins, 2018). Both leader identity and leadership development enable individuals to work with groups to facilitate change processes that enhance society (Guthrie & Jenkins, 2018). In Chapter 3, we describe the leadership learning framework (Guthrie & Jenkins, 2018) and the culturally relevant leadership learning model (Bertrand Jones et al., 2016), both of which highlight the embeddedness of reflection in leadership.

Though some consider reflection too subjective, by anchoring reflection in relevant theory and using tools such as rubrics, reflective work can be an important component for learning assessment. Reflection artifacts, such as portfolios, journals, or creative projects can also be useful for assessing learning from leadership experiences. Chapter 4 centers reflection in the leadership classroom as a key pedagogy. Similar to reflection and leadership, critical reflection is often poorly defined or broadly applied; to frame reflection in leadership learning and the possibilities for scaffolding increasingly complex reflection, Chapter 5 introduces a continuum of critical reflection. Reflective leadership educators support students by incorporating reflection into curricular and cocurricular experiences. In Chapter 6, we describe how educators can facilitate reflection and enhance their capacity through developing a reflective practice. Finally, in Chapter 7 we discuss the relationship between reflection, leadership, resilience, and mindfulness.

Turkle (2015) warned of an emerging challenge: as digital presence increases and moments of connection decrease, we lose the opportunity for self-reflection. Concurrently, the stress people experience from being inundated by negative news and world events has clarified the need for resilience in the face of stress and adversity (Grotberg, 2003a). Reflection is a powerful tool for considering experiences, including making meaning of challenging or difficult times, which is necessary for navigating a complex society and developing meaningful connections with others. As more information is available through a constantly connected global network, there is also more competition for our attention. Contemplative practices, including mindfulness, can serve as methods for reflection, as well as a complement to enhance our ability to engage in reflection. We believe reflection is critical for leadership learning; we also acknowledge there are critiques which we will address throughout the book.

This book is for anyone who cares about facilitating reflection as part of the leadership learning process. We welcome both novices and experienced educators who are interested in learning about the philosophical underpinnings of reflection and the practical application of this important pedagogy. Reflection matters for everyone. Students in K–12 and higher education need to understand the significance of reflection and develop a reflective practice that will carry through their lives. Incorporating reflection into classes, programs, and services facilitates the development of leadership knowledge. Simultaneously, educators must spend time reflecting in order to model and facilitate meaningful reflection. Finally, the academy must value reflection as part of the learning process; reflection is not value-added, but an essential component of learning. For the authors, our work, scholarship, teaching, and service has enhanced our understanding of the complexity of reflection in leadership learning, how reflection on leadership looks in practice, and how educators can further students' leadership learning through structuring and supporting reflection.

REFLECTION AND LEADERSHIP: A PRIMER

We will explore reflection and leadership in greater depth in subsequent chapters; for now, we look at the intersection of these foundational concepts. Reflection is vital for leadership learning. Guthrie and Bertrand Jones (2012) called attention to the significance of reflection for maximizing experiential leadership learning: "Leadership educators have the opportunity to guide students from merely participating in activities to making meaning of their experience. In this reflective process, students can better understand themselves and their role in the leadership process" (p. 59). Guthrie and Jenkins (2018) identified reflection as a characteristic of distinctive leadership programs that has a positive influence on leadership learning through both curricular and cocurricular experiences.

Several leadership models highlight the importance of reflection. In the leadership identity development model, a stage-based model for how students move from awareness of leadership to integration and synthesis of a leader identity, Komives, Longerbeam, Owen, Mainella, and Osteen (2006) found reflection was critical for moving through the stages, in particular during the transitions between stages. They highlighted the importance of student affairs professionals and peers, among others, in helping students reflect on their beliefs and leadership experiences (Komives et al., 2006). The social change model of leadership development (Higher Education Research Institute, 1996) includes consciousness of self which "requires an awareness of personal beliefs, values, attributes, and emotions. Self-awareness, conscious mindfulness, introspection, and continual personal reflection are foundational elements of the leadership process" (Cilente Skendall, 2017, p. 21). The social change model (Higher Education Research Institute, 1996) can be used as a tool for reflection with individuals or groups. In using the model, Early and Fincher (2017) recommended habitual reflection over episodic reflection, and they invited learners to consider mindfulness and feedback as part of developing consciousness of self. One element of the culturally relevant leadership learning model (Bertrand Jones et al., 2016) is leader identity. As a "building block that creates meaning and organizes new leadership knowledge," leader identity is "promoted through celebrations, rituals, relationships, mentoring, self-assessment, reflection, and new experiences" (Bertrand Jones et al., 2016, p. 13). Reflection is a foundational component that supports an understanding of self and leadership learning.

In addition to being a foundational element of leadership models, reflection is important for leaders to understand groups and organizations. Heifetz and Linsky (2002) wrote about the challenge of reflection and leadership using the metaphor of the balcony and the dance floor. Noting "self-reflection does not come naturally," they pointed out the importance of practicing taking a balcony perspective on events—viewing the meeting or event from a bird's eye perspective to better see patterns or understand what is going on (Heifetz & Linsky, 2002, p. 51). However, they also pointed out "if you want to affect what is happening, you must return to the dance floor" (Heifetz & Linsky, 2002, p. 53). The objective is to move iteratively between the balcony and the dance floor. By stepping back to see the impact and then returning to the experience "the goal is to come as close as you can to being in both places simultaneously" so you can observe the action, including your own, and engage (Heifetz & Linsky, 2002, p. 53). In practicing shifting between the dance floor and the balcony, learners can develop knowledge and skills for reflection while also observing patterns that impact groups and organizations.

Reflection is also important in leadership classrooms. Fritz and Guthrie (2017) found a "reflective and experiential" leadership curriculum contributed to values clarification for students (p. 53). Through a sequence of courses with reflective assignments, students reflected on their values in different ways. Fritz and Guthrie (2017) noted, "Without the classes, we are not sure participants would have been able to state their values as clearly" (p. 58). Owen (2016) pointed out "learning is core to modern approaches to leadership," and "the capacity to learn from experiences is tied directly to one's ability to analyze, integrate, and interrogate experiences in light of existing knowledge and schemas" (p. 37). This text outlines a framework for reflection in leadership learning, which can bolster the impact of reflection for leadership as an interdisciplinary and multidisciplinary pedagogy.

DEEP AND BROAD:
RESEARCHING REFLECTION IN LEADERSHIP LEARNING

As an integral component of leadership learning, reflection is included, either directly or indirectly, in many postindustrial leadership models. In order to better understand the role of reflection in leadership learning, we drew on a phenomenological study (White, 2014) that gave depth to the topic and then developed a survey to broaden the research. The *reflection in leadership learning framework* (Figure 1.1) we introduce in this chapter began with White's 2014 study and was adapted using findings from a survey conducted by the authors and a review of the literature.

Deepening Our Knowledge: Phenomenological Study

White (2014) conducted a phenomenological study of reflection in leadership learning. The study focused on how students participating in an interdisciplinary, experiential undergraduate leadership certificate utilized reflection to apply leadership theories and concepts to their lives. The study was conducted at a large, public, Research I institution in the southeast. White (2014) developed a framework based on themes that emerged from in-depth interviews with 14 students and an analysis of their reflection journals.

Participants
This study employed purposeful sampling. The population included 35 students who had completed or were completing a 120-hour experiential leadership learning course as part of an 18-credit undergraduate leadership certificate. Of the eligible students, 14 accepted the invitation to participate: two recent graduates, 10 seniors, and two juniors. The par-

ticipants included nine White women, one Black woman, two Latina women, and two White men; this was representative of the students pursuing the leadership certificate. The 120-hour leadership experiences included internships and service-learning placements at local and international nonprofit agencies, local and state government offices, and on-campus departments.

Data Collection

The study included two in-depth, semistructured interviews with each of the 14 participants. Each interview lasted 45 to 90 minutes. The interviews focused on students' perception of reflection and leadership as well as how students applied leadership theories and concepts through reflection. Interviews were recorded and transcribed verbatim. Prior to the study, as part of the course, participants completed 30 one-page journal entries about their leadership learning experience, and these were also included in the analysis.

Data Analysis

The transcripts and journal entries were analyzed using NVivo 10. White (2014) coded 28 transcripts and more than 400 pages of reflection journals, engaging in an iterative process of qualitative analysis. After completing first and second cycle coding (Saldaña, 2013), several themes emerged. Students talked about learning to reflect, reflecting upon leadership concepts, and applying what they learned from their reflection (White, 2014). The themes were organized into elements of reflection in leadership learning: grounding ideas, support structures, and outcomes.

Broadening Our Understanding: Survey

In order to understand reflection in leadership learning broadly, we developed a survey which was administered to students at a large, public, Research I institution in the southeast in 2017 and 2018.

Instrument

The survey was adapted with permission from an instrument used by Mitchell et al. (2015) that looked at "the relationship between reflective practices in college service-learning programs and alumni's current reflective practices" (p. 49). The survey questions included both open- and closed-ended items that asked about reflection, leadership, reflective practices, how students learned to reflect, what supports or inhibits reflection, people with whom students reflect, reflective spaces, and what students gain from reflection. Because of limited research on the intersection of leadership and reflection, a number of questions were open-ended to invite a multitude of responses.

Sample

Data collection took place between spring 2017 and spring 2018 when an anonymous survey link was emailed to students in curricular and cocurricular leadership learning programs. The survey was also an option in an established subject pool through the College of Education for five consecutive semesters (spring 2017–summer 2018), and students who completed the survey through the subject pool received extra credit for their participation. There were 601 students who completed the survey; students who did not complete the survey were excluded from the analysis.

Demographic Profiles

Of the 601 respondents, 74% identified as women, 26% identified as men, and less than 1% identified as trans*, genderqueer, or nonbinary. The racial and ethnic makeup included 66% White, 13% Hispanic/Latinx, 10% Black or African American, 8% Two or More Races, 2% Asian, and less than 1% Native Hawaiian or other Pacific Islander, nonresident alien, or prefer not to disclose. The survey focused on undergraduates with a distribution of 10% first years, 24% sophomores, 32% juniors, 31% seniors, and 3% graduate students. Of the 16 colleges at the institution, 13 were represented with four colleges comprising the majority of respondents: human sciences (28%), arts and sciences (19%), education (20%), and social sciences (10%).

Data Analysis

Responses were collected using Qualtrics and exported to Excel. Incomplete responses were removed. Scale-based and closed-ended items were uploaded to Stata for an analysis of descriptive statistics. Open-ended responses were uploaded to NVivo 12 Pro where multiple researchers engaged in an iterative and inductive process of coding responses. Codes were clustered together based on emerging patterns in the data.

REFLECTION IN LEADERSHIP LEARNING FRAMEWORK

Learners engage in reflection in many settings, whether as part of a structured class assignment, through a cocurricular learning opportunity, or in the context of their daily lives. Students may engage in reflective thinking on their own or with others. There are a number of methods and activities that support reflection. Regardless of the setting, company, or methods, reflection is rarely simple. As reflective thinking often produces more questions than answers, this type of intentional rumination requires guidance, nurturing, and practice over time. Through consistent reflection, learners may enhance their capacity for reflective thought. The reflection process is neither linear nor cyclical; it is iterative. We illustrate the complex, relational process of reflection in leadership learning using a tree. As we elaborate on the reflection in leadership learning framework (Figure 1.1), we highlight the parallels between the complexity of reflection in leadership learning and the intricate systems that comprise these living organisms.

Overview

In many ways, the iterative process of reflection mirrors the growth and development of a tree. Roots anchor a tree to the ground. They provide stability and absorb water which is crucial for sustaining life (Hirons & Thomas, 2018). Recently, scientists discovered that in many forests, the root systems of trees are intertwined which enables the systems to "communicate" in order to more effectively support the health of the community (Wohlleben, 2015). Similarly, the roots in the framework represent the functions that ground reflection in both theory and practice. These elements provide stability which enables the growth and development of the individual and the community. The trunk of a tree is strengthened over time; in response to stresses from wind and other elements, the trunk repairs itself and develops resilience (Wohlleben, 2015). When trees are able to rely on one another, they can put energy into growing taller (Wohlleben, 2015). In the framework (Figure 1.1), the trunk represents support structures provided by educators, peers, or family. These support structures bolster students in order to enhance reflective capacity and facilitate learning. The relational element of reflection in leadership learning supports a more resilient community and provides energy for individual, group, and community development. In the crown of the tree, the leaves receive sunlight to engage in the process of photosynthesis which provides nutrients that are carried back to the roots (Hirons & Thomas, 2018). Without a sufficient crown, the tree cannot nourish itself (Wohlleben, 2015). As an iterative process, learning that results from reflection is not an endpoint, but informs subsequent learning and development. The outcomes inform interactions with support structures and grounding elements for future reflective practice.

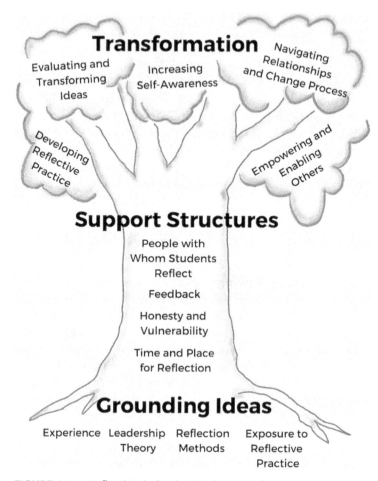

FIGURE 1.1. Reflection in leadership learning framework.

Applicability to Various Contexts

Both the phenomenological study by White (2014) and the survey were conducted at one large, public, Research I institution. Several studies of leadership acknowledged the potential limitations of qualitative research while also highlighting the importance of qualitative research in exploring complex aspects of leadership (Eich, 2008; Haber-Curran & Tillapaugh, 2013; Komives, Owen, Longerbeam, Mainella, & Osteen, 2005). Based on the context for the research, this text primarily addresses reflection in leadership learning from a Western lens, and more research should be conducted to explore these concepts globally. It is our hope readers can determine how elements of the framework might translate to their leadership learning contexts.

ROOTS: GROUNDING IDEAS

As "the 'hidden branches' of a tree," roots "are vital for the development and persistence of trees" (Hirons & Thomas, 2018, p. 141). Roots absorb water and nutrients, and "the tree's stability is dependent on the roots' capacity to provide anchorage" (Hirons & Thomas, 2018, p. 141). Much like the roots are the foundation for the tree, the grounding elements form the base of the reflection in leadership learning framework. As seen in Figure 1.2., these components anchor reflection in theory and practice, which prepares students for sustained growth. Educators have both the opportunity and the responsibility to incorporate these elements into curricular and cocurricular leadership learning. Not only can reflection support leadership learning in specific settings, but engaging students in reflection can develop the foundation necessary for a lifelong reflection.

Experience

Experience is a central component of and catalyst for reflective learning (Dewey, 1933; Kolb, 1984; Schön, 1983). Each day, students have experiences that provide occasions for reflection. On the continuum of experiential leadership learning, at one end are daily interactions students have including encounters with peers, family, administrators, community members, and social media; at the other end are intentionally structured curricular or cocurricular experiences including service-learning, internships,

FIGURE 1.2.   Reflection in leadership learning framework: Grounding ideas.

and research. Between unstructured interactions and structured learning experiences, there are a multiple opportunities for engagement including classroom activities, student organizations, outdoor education, and gaming simulations, among others. In some cases, students have structured opportunities for reflection, or they may have casual conversations that engage them in reflective thinking.

In experiential learning, despite having less control of situations once students leave the classroom, educators can assist students in setting up and reflecting upon experiences in order to maximize learning. It is also important to consider the value of challenges students encounter through experiential learning. White (2014) found most participants encountered challenges during their leadership experiences including lack of direction from supervisors, frustration with established processes, lack of confidence, or struggling to balance competing priorities. However, most students also acknowledged how they grew through difficult circumstances. In one example, shortly after a student arrived at her international service placement, the director was removed for embezzling funds. She observed other interns "check out" but said reflection helped her process the experience and "gave it purpose at times where I felt like there wasn't purpose." Especially when experiences are challenging or frustrating, educators should engage students in reflection. Experience can be a catalyst for reflection, and leadership theory provides a body of work to which students can anchor their experiences.

Leadership Theory

Leadership education is both interdisciplinary and multidisciplinary (Guthrie & Jenkins, 2018). Contrary to industrial leadership theories, which equate leadership with positionality, Rost (1993), who built on the work of Burns (1978), advanced a postindustrial definition of leadership as *"an influence relationship among leaders and followers who intend real changes that reflect their mutual purposes"* (p. 102, emphasis in original). Deep reflection does not happen spontaneously, but more often in response to new information or addressing feelings of discomfort. By engaging with leadership theories, particularly theories that challenge existing or popular notions of leadership, learners can reframe their understanding of leadership through reflection. This can include formal theory, communicated in a classroom, or informal theory, developed through experience (Schön, 1983). White (2014) found most participants struggled to recall the names of specific theories, however in sharing stories about their learning, students demonstrated knowledge and application of leadership theories. By learning the formal theories, many students shifted their perspective from an industrial, hierarchical, leader-centric understanding of leadership to a more postindustrial conception of leadership that valued relationships and collaborative work. For many of the students, a significant takeaway from reflecting on their leadership coursework and experiences was reframing leadership from a position to a process (White, 2014). One of the participants was clear: "*Everybody* can learn how to be a leader. I feel like that was definitely one of *the first* lessons that I learned." As students learn about leadership theory and practice, they prepare a base of knowledge, develop skills, and reflect on their values; this sets the stage for applying their leadership knowledge, skills, and values in practice. A shared understanding of leadership and the process of leader development also provides a common language for students and instructors (Guthrie & Jenkins, 2018), which can facilitate providing feedback and evaluating reflection artifacts.

Reflection Methods

Reflection methods are multifaceted and range from straightforward to complex, entry level to cognitively challenging, and individual to group oriented. Reflection can be as straightforward as a conversation between an educator and a student, as complex as a scaffolded multiweek portfolio project, as collaborative as a group presentation about perspective transformation resulting from community engagement, or as individual as writing in a journal. Methods for reflection support the spectrum of cognitive processes (Anderson & Krathwohl, 2000)—learners may remember factual knowledge from a 1-hour workshop, apply a skill learned through a service-learning project, or evaluate an internship experience through a capstone project. Additionally, there are multiple methods for reflection. In this text and the companion manual (Volpe White, Guthrie, & Torres, 2019, we group reflection activities into six methods: contemplative, creative, digital, discussion, narrative, and written.

White (2014) found discussion was a preferred strategy for reflection: all participants mentioned reflective class discussion, and many talked about structured conversations in programs, meetings with trusted mentors, or informal gatherings with friends or roommates. Although not a preferred method, most students acknowledged the value of written reflection in academic settings (White, 2014). Among creative methods for reflection, students utilized photography, poetry, painting, media production, and music (White, 2014). Responses to the survey mirrored what White (2014) found: students preferred active reflection and discussion. Students were presented with methods for reflection and asked to indicate the utility of each. The method with the highest mean response was physical activity (e.g., running, walking, yoga) and the lowest mean responses were blogging and social media. Moderately useful methods included informal dialogue with peers, creative activities (e.g., painting, dancing), and meditation. Although the content and cognitive process may be more significant than the method, having a broad range of options for reflection may support students' willingness to reflect. For educators preparing students to learn from experience, an effective reflection plan should include multiple methods of reflection (Ash & Clayton, 2009; Eyler, 2001).

Exposure to Reflective Practice

There is some disagreement as to whether reflection "is a natural and familiar process" (Daudelin, 1996, p. 37) or requires intentional engagement (Heifetz & Linksky, 2002). In the survey, participants were asked "How did you learn to reflect?" The most common response was observing or engaging with other people such as family, parents, and mentors. The next highest response was school. The third largest group included participants who said reflection "just came naturally" or "I taught myself." Less common responses included learning from experiences or challenging situations, journaling, physical activity, religion or spirituality, meditation, creative outlets, or online resources such as YouTube videos. Curricular and cocurricular leadership learning programs have the opportunity to engage students in reflective practice, perhaps for the first time they are conscious of reflection.

Students had mixed reactions to assigned reflection (also referred to as compulsory, required, or forced reflection), however, they generally valued being asked to reflect upon experiences they may not have considered on their own (White, 2012; White, 2014). White (2014) had one student express both sentiments simultaneously:

> I can't say I enjoy the journals because it is homework. It is sitting there writing but it's a good way to know what my thought process is. I don't sit there and I think "Oh no that paragraph wasn't good. I'm going to rewrite that." I just I sit there and I write my thoughts. So I guess I do enjoy that in a way. It does take time out of my day, which I don't enjoy, but it's nice to kind of sit and reflect.

One study of honesty in critically reflective essays found students sometimes elaborated on experiences to meet assignment criteria or word counts (Maloney, Tai, Lo, Molloy, & Ilic, 2013). Although not something students always appreciate in the moment, with practice students may find reflection feels more natural or they are more appreciative of reflection.

TRUNK: SUPPORT STRUCTURES

The trunk of a tree is composed of layers which support growth and sustain life (Hirons & Thomas, 2018). The support structures (Figure 1.3) that make up the trunk enable students to reflect on their experiences moving through the iterative process of recalling, analyzing, synthesizing, and evaluating knowledge, skills, and values. Although educators have some influence over the degree to which the grounding elements are incorporated into experiential learning, they play a central role in the support structures.

People With Whom Students Reflect

Though reflection may seem like an individual process, Dewey (1933) argued reflection happens in community. Taylor (2009) found authentic, trusting relationships made it possible for more in-depth reflection, and mentoring is one component that influences student's potential for socially responsible leadership (Dugan & Komives, 2007). As discussion is a preferred reflection strategy for students, it is not surprising the people with whom students reflect play a significant role in their leadership

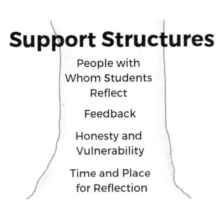

FIGURE 1.3.   Reflection in leadership learning framework—Support structures.

learning. Although some students had one person who was a trusted confidant, many students identified multiple people with whom they reflected, often for different reasons or in different situations (White, 2014). Students may gravitate toward people who model authenticity or create a safe or welcoming space for reflection (White, 2014). Though sometimes students planned intentional one-on-one meetings to reflect with an internship supervisor or trusted mentor, other times reflection seemed like a natural byproduct of meaningful conversation (White, 2014). As part of the survey, students were asked to identify people with whom they reflect. Among the top responses were parent or guardian (40%), friend (21%), significant other (9%), sibling (7%), mentor (3%), and professor, faculty, or instructor (3%). Respondents also identified other people as significant for reflection: 27% said conversation, dialogue, discussion, feedback, or prompts from others enhanced their ability to reflect. The people with whom students reflect are significant for promoting and supporting reflection as well as providing feedback.

Feedback

As students described the people with whom they reflected, one of the most valuable roles they played was providing feedback. Leadership learning is a complex and iterative process that requires both intense self-reflection as well as feedback from others (Boyd & Williams, 2010; Conger, 1992; Komives et al., 2005). White (2014) found participants sought feedback to gauge performance, modify action, assess learning, and help see something they did not realize, whether it was a lack of confidence, an overcommitted schedule, or a specific task for their internship. Students noted feedback was not only about improvement; they also valued receiving feedback on things they did well. One student described the value of feedback succinctly: "Feedback allows for more thought to be introduced, more ideas to come forward to propel an idea or solution" (White, 2014). In a study of reflection methods for service-learning, Sturgill and Motley (2014) found sharing feedback on reflections regularly rather than waiting until the end of the semester allowed faculty to direct students' thinking in instructive ways. Eyler and Giles (1999) noted coaching and feedback were important for all reflection, but particularly significant for critical reflection. Receiving feedback from others may contribute to increased self-awareness because students learn about themselves, and in this way feedback may serve as a catalyst for additional reflection and development. The ability to give and receive feedback is closely connected to honesty and vulnerability.

Honesty and Vulnerability

Honest and vulnerable reflection is cultivated over time through developing trust and creating spaces that invite transparency. Students value spaces where they feel comfortable sharing honest thoughts and feelings. In the survey, several students highlighted the importance of honesty for enhancing reflection. White and Guthrie (2016) found "through intentionally structuring a learning environment conducive to reflection, leadership educators can increase opportunities for authentic and vulnerable reflection" (p. 72). We cannot tout the benefits of reflection without acknowledging it can sometimes be difficult, confusing, or painful. Students may avoid reflecting because they are not prepared to address a difficult situation or topic. In the survey, respondents identified three primary inhibitors of reflection: being busy or doing other things, distractions, and emotions or feelings. Some of the emotions or feelings respondents described included denial, fear, stress, anxiety, depression, and being upset or overwhelmed. Elaborating on their fears, students wrote about fear of facing reality, fear of failure, and fear of self-discovery. Conversely, a small group of students described how stress or negative emotions could enhance their reflection. Students may also resist honest reflection when they are being graded and do not want to risk being viewed negatively by instructors or facilitators (Eyler & Giles, 1999; Fernsten & Fernsten, 2005; O'Connell & Dyment, 2011). Educators can enhance the possibility of honesty and vulnerability by creating environments that feel safe for participants to express authentic reflections. To the degree they are comfortable, educators can support authentic reflection by sharing their own reflections and modeling honesty and vulnerability. In some cases, the ability to have honest and vulnerable reflection can be influenced by the time and place for reflection.

Time and Place for Reflection

Time for reflection includes frequency, occasion, and even season of life. Many students described the importance of reflection but lamented not making reflection a priority (White, 2014). White (2014) found time could be a barrier for reflection because students felt like their days were too full or because reflection was subsumed by other priorities. In the survey, one of the most significant inhibitors for reflection was being busy or doing other things. On the other hand, some students set specific times for reflection, such as mornings, evenings, or a specific day of the week. Schön's (1983) reflection-in-action encouraged professionals to reflect consistently in their work. Heifetz and Linsky (2002) described the iterative shift between the balcony and the dance floor. However, developing the ability to engage in reflective thought amidst other distractions or activities takes practice, and for students beginning their leadership learning journey there may be times and places that are more conducive for reflection. Educators can support students by setting aside time for reflection. This may take many different forms including a reflective writing assignment or discussion in a class, a creative activity as part of a student organization retreat, or infusing one-on-one meetings with reflective questions. By designating time for reflection, students are invited to connect what they are learning to areas of interest and prioritize learning and reflection. Time is at a premium, both personally and in the classroom, however, reflection adds value to the learning experience and making reflection a priority signals its value for leadership learning.

Closely connected to time for reflection is the place for reflection. Place can include a specific setting, such as a campus green or a beach, and it can also refer to how educators set up classroom spaces to invite reflection. As part of the survey, students were invited to submit a photo of or describe a reflective place. The most frequently described places were outside or in nature, such as beach or ocean, or students' rooms. A sense of place can also refer to how educators set up spaces for reflection. Some of the practices which facilitate meaningful leadership learning environments in the classroom include engaging with instructors who value and encourage reflection; having small, discussion-based classes; arranging the chairs in a circle to promote interaction among equals; and engaging with diverse peers (White & Guthrie, 2016). Beyond a classroom setting, educators can work with campus partners to create spaces that invite people to pause and reflect. These may include outdoor green spaces, clusters of tables and chairs in lobbies or academic buildings, or a labyrinth.

CROWN: TRANSFORMATION

The crown of the tree is made up a "conglomeration of leaves" that "have the fundamental task of intercepting light;" the light, along with water and carbon dioxide, provides fuel for photosynthesis (Hirons & Thomas, 2018, p. 77). The crown of the tree is made up of transformative outcomes (Figure 1.4) which represent the generative power of reflection. Students nourish themselves through reflection and create positive change through self-development and interactions with others. It is important to note not all students who reflect on leadership experiences will attain all these outcomes, and there may be other transformative aspects that result from reflection. The common thread between these outcomes is they support the development of students as engaged and effective leaders in their communities.

Figure 1.4.   Reflection in leadership learning framework—Transformation.

Increasing Self-Awareness

Self-awareness is a foundational concept of emotionally intelligent leadership (Shankman, Allen, & Haber-Curran, 2015) that is developed by seeking feedback and reflecting in order to become more aware of capacities and opportunities for development. Almost all of the students interviewed by White (2014) described self-awareness as an outcome of reflection in leadership learning. Several participants noted the role of feedback in developing self-awareness; by being more aware of themselves, they also became more aware of their interactions with others (White, 2014). Another element of self-awareness was self-care and being able to articulate needs without apology (White, 2014). One student recognized the importance of separating herself from her work: "I put in *so many hours*. Like 70 hours a week and a lot of that is on my own time ... I need to find a balance or else I will not feel full and I want to feel full." When asked what she meant by "full," she responded, "Mind, body, soul. Taking care of myself" (White, 2014). Increased awareness may also support metacognition or the ability of students to be aware of and in control of their thought processes (Fogarty & Pete, 2018). One student described the ability to reflect and then reflect on her reflection; other students described developing awareness of what they gained from reflection (White, 2014). By learning to reflect, engaging in reflection, and considering how they learn from reflection, students may develop metacognitive skills.

Navigating Relationships and Change Processes

Two important processes, which are closely connected, are navigating relationships and change processes; through reflection on leadership learning, participants felt better equipped for both (White, 2014). This supports leadership models including the social change model (Higher Education Research Institute, 1996), leadership identity development model (Komives et al., 2006), leadership challenge (Kouzes & Posner, 2007), relational model of leadership (Komives, Lucas, & McMahon, 2013), and culturally relevant leadership learning model (Bertrand Jones et al., 2016), all of which have a relational or collaborative element and support change processes. Understanding leadership as a relational process, students valued the opportunity to reflect on relationships and their roles in groups (White, 2014). All participants described trying to facilitate a change process, whether making the recruitment process for a student organization more transparent, shifting the culture of a sorority from philanthropy to service, proposing a new fundraising plan for a nonprofit organization, or reorganizing processes at an internship site (White, 2014). In many cases, students were met with resistance or questions, and their understanding of the change process allowed them to balance frustrations with taking risk and persevering (White, 2014). In some cases they achieved their goals and in other cases the change did not take root; in many cases students reflected on how they managed the process and engaged with others (White, 2014).

Empowering and Enabling Others

Postindustrial leadership focuses not on a singular leader figure but on leadership as a mutually beneficial process (Rost, 1993). Through reflection, White (2014) found many participants shifted from thinking about leadership as a titled position to thinking about leadership as an opportunity to encourage others in their development. This echoes the last two stages of the leadership identity development model (Komives et al., 2006) where students move from considering leadership as a position to focusing on meaningful engagement with others and the long-term sustainability of organizations. Particularly in their journals, students talked about how they had been empowered and enabled; in turn, they wanted to empower and enable others. Kouzes and Posner (2018) described the importance of fostering collaboration and strengthening others as part of enabling others to act. They acknowledged this "paradox of power: you become most powerful when you give your power away" (Kouzes & Posner, 2018, p. 202). Participants described experiences at philanthropy events, student organization meetings, and group projects where they reframed the experience: instead of being in charge, they developed capacity in others. Another way students manifested empowerment and support was through mentoring peers (White, 2014). Although some participants admitted to still focusing on their own role or legacy, many students reflected on the process of learning how to collaborate with and empower others (White, 2014).

Developing Reflective Practice

Reflection is not necessarily intuitive, and asking students to reflect without context or preparation may result in confusion or frustration (Owen-Smith, 2018). Some students recalled reflecting at youth group, camp, or around the dinner table with family, but for almost half of the participants, an outcome of their leadership coursework was discovering reflection and learning how to reflect (White, 2014). Engaging in reflection with others helped students see the value of reflection. As a result of their leadership learning experiences, some participants said reflection came more naturally, and they also identified reflection as a beneficial practice for their life or career (White, 2014). In particular, students who were approaching graduation described the importance of reflecting during the transition. However, recognizing the importance of reflection does not always translate into prioritizing reflective practice. Mitchell et al. (2015) found while alumni of service-learning programs understood the value of reflective practice they may not always make reflection a priority in their lives. Although some of the participants did not consider themselves to be reflective people, and admittedly did not set aside time for reflection, most students identified experience and reflection as significant components of leadership learning (White, 2014).

Evaluating and Transforming Ideas

Evaluating and transforming ideas is an significant outcome of reflection in leadership learning. Although the assumption of this element could be seen as underscoring the entire framework, it is important to name this as an outcome of reflection. Mezirow (2012) described how reflection contributed to transformative learning by challenging assumptions or presuppositions. Ash and Clayton (2009) detailed how reflection facilitates evaluating and transforming ideas: "It *generates* learning (articulating questions, confronting bias, examining causality, contrasting theory with practice, pointing to systemic issues), *deepens* learning (challenging simplistic conclusions, inviting alternative perspectives, asking "why" iteratively), and *documents* learning (producing tangible expressions of new understandings for evaluation)" (p. 27). Not every reflection experience will lead to an epiphany, but reflection should encourage participants to assess their actions and beliefs which may lead to transformation.

White (2014) found almost half of the participants described perspective changes as a result of reflection. Several students described how their understanding of leadership shifted from "leaders as the people in charge" to "leadership as a process of supporting others and adapting to change" (White, 2014). Students also identified perspective changes in their lives (White, 2014). For example, one student described how reflection lead him to change his voter registration:

> I feel like I was just a Republican because my parents were. But then I figured out for myself what are their values, what are their beliefs, what are my values, my beliefs. I figured out I really don't agree with what they're saying.

In the survey, students were asked to describe an aha moment or a time when a perspective or belief they held was transformed as a result of reflection. Some of the topics included observing how behaviors helped or hindered academic success; understanding self and relationships with others; and realizing a career path was or was not a good fit. A few students wrote about changing their perspective on a social issue such as gun laws, abortion, marriage equality, climate change, or gender roles, among others. One student noted, "After the Stoneman Douglass incident my conservative views have transformed. Not fully but I do actively place myself in other people's shoes, causing me to alter my views." Another student wrote,

> I used to believe it was wrong for minority groups to receive special advantages over the majority, because that seemed unfair to me. It was only after further reflection and actual research that I concluded that the playing field isn't fair in the first place if you are a minority.

A third respondent said, "My view on the current situation with our president was not a very positive one, but with reflection with my peers, they were able to give me some insight into some positive aspects and somewhat changed my perspective." Whether about something straightforward or a complex social issue, many respondents were able to describe how reflection led to evaluating their beliefs or attitudes. Owen (2016) described how deeper levels of reflection linked to leadership could facilitate transformative actions for individuals, groups, and communities. Given the potential for reflection to challenge learners to evaluate their beliefs and assumptions, it is important to consider how reflection may lead to transformation.

EXPLORING TENSIONS AND POSSIBILITIES FOR REFLECTION IN LEADERSHIP LEARNING

In the mid-1900s, reflection was framed as a radical approach to education. In *Teaching as a Subversive Activity*, Postman and Weingartner (1969) critiqued a system of education that simply transmitted information and instead proposed strategies for educating learners capable of addressing complex situations. Freire's *Pedagogy of the Oppressed* (1970/1996) highlighted reflection as a tool for liberation: "But human activity consists of action and reflection: it is praxis; it is transformation of the world" (p. 106). Kemmis (1985) pointed out that against a background of the belief in modern industrial thought "a book about reflection is a subversive text. It is, at least, an affirmation of the enlightenment spirit that human thoughts can strain against the shackles of mass culture, perhaps even break free" (p. 140). However, as reflection has become more mainstream, it has "moved away from those radical roots" and "in the process, its radical potential was subsumed by individualistic, rather than situated, understandings of practice" (Kilminster, Zukas, Bradbury, & Frost, 2010, p. 2). There is a clear tension between reflection as a radical and transformative approach to education and reflection as a mainstream tool that engages learners as individuals without the benefit of thinking broadly and deeply about the world.

As we consider the role of reflection in leadership learning, we look to voices in education (Brookfield, 2017), service-learning (Mitchell, 2008), social work (Fook, 2016), and other disciplines calling for reflection that integrates critical theory and moves beyond individual benefits toward action for change. Reflection is a powerful tool for learning, and it can also be a means to create positive change in society; this can only be enhanced through coupling reflection and leadership learning. Leadership needs reflection for students to develop cognitive complexity and respond to adaptive challenges; reflection needs leadership as an action-oriented discipline that empowers and enables learners to develop individually and in community to create positive change. Reflection in leadership learning creates possibilities for learning and engagement which could not be so without both. Together, reflection and leadership learning have synergistic possibilities: by embedding reflection in leadership learning, we enhance the capacity of learners to engage in an inclusive and justice-oriented leadership process.

CHAPTER 2

REFLECTION DEFINED

In the broadest sense, reflection is the process by which people make meaning of experience. Philosophers and educators have argued experience alone is insufficient for learning; it is through reflection that we analyze our experiences and engage in learning in order to synthesize knowledge. Reflection is different than thinking about something that happened; it requires cognitive and affective complexity to consider past experiences, draw conclusions, infer meaning, and consider applications for the future. Mezirow (2012) identified learning as being at the core of the human experience: "A defining condition of being human is our urgent need to understand and order the meaning of our experience, to integrate it with what we know to avoid the threat of chaos" (p. 73). Reflection is an integral part of learning.

Similar to leadership, one of the critiques of reflection is it lacks a clear definition. Although it may be beneficial for reflection as a concept to have operational latitude, the lack of clarity can be problematic particularly when educators ask students to reflect with the assumption students know what this means. If educators cannot conceptualize reflection, it is unreasonable to expect students asked to reflect can do so without coaching through the process or clear expectations (Beauchamp, 2015). Another critique of reflection is it is too "touchy feely." Ash and Clayton (2009) explained that to elevate reflection, "first requires that we make clear its meaning as an integrative, analytical, capacity-building process rather than as a superficial exercise in navel-gazing" (p. 28). Reflection is a complex, multifaceted concept; when executed with intentionality, reflection enhances leadership learning.

Thinking to Transform: Reflection in Leadership Learning
pp. 25–43
Copyright © 2019 by Information Age Publishing
All rights of reproduction in any form reserved.

Reflection neither consists solely of activities incorporated into curricular and cocurricular experiences; nor is reflection purely a theoretical exercise in examining abstract ideas. The richness of reflection for leadership educators lies in pairing experiences with theory-driven reflections to facilitate student learning and development. The question becomes: how do we make reflection accessible to novices and worthy of the time and attention of educators, while also elevating reflection to the high standard of thinking and complexity required to shift perspectives and lead to the integration of new knowledge? Simultaneously, how do we shift reflection from an individual exercise in knowing and thinking to a collective experience that results in positive social change? This chapter explores the complexity of reflection as a philosophy, a pedagogy and instructional strategy, a way to assess learning, and a collection of methods that facilitate learning processes.

PHILOSOPHICAL GROUNDING

The history of reflective thinking is long with some authors pointing to the origins as Confucius (Liu, 2015) or Aristotle (Hatton & Smith, 1995; Ng & Tan, 2009). Webster-Wright (2013) noted, "Socrates' affirmation of the value of 'the examined life' traces reflective practice to antiquity" (p. 557). Dewey's (1933) philosophy is often cited as the seminal work on reflection; however, historical developments related to reflection are not easy to trace. Disciplinary adoptions, adaptations of theories, and simultaneous developments have resulted in a web of related works that make up the body of literature on reflection. The historical grounding in philosophy, and the theoretical works which frame reflection, are important to situate reflection as a concept. Reflection is often reduced to activities without a broader understanding of the undergirding theory. Although there are situations that call for reflection activities that are more introductory or surface level, the power of reflection comes from a grounding in philosophical approaches to thinking and learning that situate reflection as a pedagogy. This section is not inclusive of all writers who discuss reflection, but it includes authors whose work has influenced the development of reflection as an educational pedagogy.

Reflective Thinking in Education: John Dewey

Dewey (1933), who drew from philosophers including Aristotle, Plato, Confucius, Buddha, Lao Tzu, and Solomon (Houston, 1988), maintained reflection was the goal of education. He distinguished reflection from other forms of thought – stream of consciousness, imagination, and belief—by the way reflective thought built upon successive thoughts in sequence, lead to an outcome or application, and relied on personal investigation through inquiry. He also distinguished reflection by the state of doubt or confusion that prompted thinking and the act of searching for materials which would resolve the doubt. Dewey (1933) cautioned against jumping to conclusions, failing to test ideas, or generalizing, and identified three attitudes that supported reflective thought: open-mindedness, whole-heartedness, and responsibility.

Dewey's (1933) definition of reflection is regularly cited; he conceived reflection as *"active, persistent, and careful consideration of any belief of supposed form of knowledge in light of the ground that support it and the further conclusions to which it tends"* (p. 9, emphasis in original). Dewey (1933) noted reflective thought is neither simple nor easy, but "demand for the solution of a perplexity is the steadying and guiding factor in the entire process of reflection" (p. 14). Like many models that frame reflection as cyclical, Dewey (1933) imagined learners moving through a cycle and gaining depth with each pass.

Reflection-in-Action: Donald Schön

In his exploration of the reflective practitioner, Schön (1983) distinguished between two modes of reflection: technical rationality, a hierarchical model that relies on learned professions to generate knowledge which is "specialized, firmly bounded, scientific, and standardized" (p. 23), and reflection-in-action, where professionals reflect on actions, ideas, and criticisms to restructure future actions. Technical rationality holds research as separate from practice and devalues learning that occurs in practice because it may lack rigor. Reflection-in-action is stimulated by "puzzling, or troubling, or interesting phenomenon with which the individual is trying to deal" (Schön, 1983, p. 50) and shifts practitioners from applying knowledge derived from "experts" to creating expert knowledge through their work. In the face of unanticipated consequences, either positive or negative, reflective practitioners dissect the actions and outcomes, engaging with the problem and moving beyond technical conceptions (Schön, 1983). In this way, reflection-in-action becomes research in practice and develops reflective practitioners. The focus of reflection-in-action may include systems, patterns, behaviors, situations, or a specific problem. Reflection-in-action is a featured approach to reflection in nurse education, teacher education, and social work (Thompson & Pascal, 2012).

Reflection in Experiential Learning: David Kolb

Kolb's (1984) work is used broadly to inform experiential learning. Kolb's (1984) cycle of experiential learning was grounded in the work of other theorists who addressed reflection. Lewin's (1951) action research emphasized concrete experience based on feedback processes. Dewey (1933) was more explicit in identifying the role of feedback processes in development. Piaget (1970) described the movement of individuals from a concrete phenomenal view in infancy to reflective internalized knowing in adulthood. For Kolb (1984), experiential learning had the potential to go beyond a set of practices to be "a program for profoundly re-creating our personal lives and social system" (p. 18), and experience complemented theory in the learning process as a "holistic integrative perspective on learning that combines experience, perception, cognition, and behavior" (p. 21). Kolb (1984) identified six characteristics of experiential learning: learning is a process, learning is grounded in experience, learning requires resolving opposing ideas, learning is holistic and requires adaptation, learning entails person and environment interaction, and the process of learning is one of knowledge creation.

The cycle of experiential learning codified a process by which learners observed the world, reflected on experiences, drew conclusions based on reflection, and experimented or acted on their conclusions (Kolb, 1984). Rather than a linear progression, the process is cyclical; learners can enter the cycle at any point and continue iteratively through the process developing greater knowledge and experience with each pass. The cycle of experiential learning (Kolb, 1984) includes four phases: concrete experience (engaging in new experiences with an emphasis on feelings), reflective observation (understanding experiences by watching versus thinking or acting), abstract conceptualization (thinking, particularly to understand concepts using logic), and active experimentation (applying information and influencing people or situations). Regarding Kolb's (1984) cycle, Stevens and Cooper (2009) described reflection as the "engine that moves the learning cycle along its path to further learning, action, and more reflection" (p. 24). Without reflection, there is no new understanding of actions.

Reflection for Transformative Learning: Jack Mezirow

Transformative learning is a theory of adult education focused on perspective transformation. Mezirow's (1978a, 1978b) early work on adult education focused on women returning to community college following a hiatus; his research team revealed a 10-phase, nonsequential process of

learning initiated by a disorienting dilemma and resulted in the reinte-
gration of a new perspective (Baumgartner, 2012; Kitchenham, 2008).
Since 1978, transformative learning theory has expanded, evolved, and
been refined (Baumgartner, 2012; Kitchenham, 2008) through the influence of theorists including Kuhn (1962), Freire (1970), and Habermas
(1971, 1984; Kitchenham, 2008). Drawing on earlier scholarship, the first
comprehensive publication of transformative learning theory was introduced in 1991; in this publication, Mezirow (1991) presented the theory
as interdisciplinary and rooted in constructivism, humanism, and critical
social theory (Cranton & Taylor, 2012). Building on more than 30 years of
work, Mezirow (2012) described transformation theory as:

> The process by which we transform our taken-for-granted frames of refer-
> ence (meaning perspectives, habits of mind, mind-sets) to make them more
> inclusive, discriminating, open, emotionally capable of change, and reflec-
> tive so that they may generate beliefs and opinions that will prove more true
> or justified to guide action. (p. 76)

Not all learning is transformative; learning is contextual and transformation theory focuses on "how we learn to negotiate and act on our own
purposes, values, feelings, and meanings rather than those we have
uncritically assimilated from others" (Mezirow, 2012, p. 76). Reflection is
foundational for transformative learning, particularly critical reflection
on assumptions (Mezirow, 2012). How educators and learners approach
reflection in leadership learning will be influenced by their perspective.

CONSTRUCTIVISM

A perspective "is a lens for how a person makes sense of the surrounding
world" that is shaped by background and experience (Biddix, 2018, p. 45).
Constructivism, also called social constructivism, is a philosophical perspective and research paradigm. Constructivism holds a relativist ontol-
ogy: "when considering what can be known, entities are matters of
definition and convention; they exist only in the minds of the persons con-
templating them. They do not 'really' exist" (Lincoln & Guba, 2013, p.
39). In other words, despite attempts to define intangible entities such as
"leadership" or "reflection," the conceptualization depends largely on
who is doing the defining. Epistemology describes the relationships
between the knower and what is known. In constructivism, "the relationship between the knower and the knowable (to-be-known) is highly
person- and context-specific" (Lincoln & Guba, 2013, p. 40). This
relationship is mediated by experience, identity, and context. Knowledge
created is context specific.

The philosophical perspective held by educational philosophers who wrote about reflection runs the gamut. Dewey (1933) aligned more with pragmatism (Maddux & Donnett, 2015). Schön (1983) equated technical rationality with positivist epistemology and described the tension between engaging in technical, positivist ways of knowing as opposed to exploring and reflecting on potentially more rich but less rigorous information gained through experience; this dichotomy highlights the tension between positivism and constructivism as they relate to reflection. Mezirow (2012) embraced constructivism: "As there are no fixed truths or totally definitive knowledge, and because circumstances change, the human condition may be best understood as a continuous effort to nego-tiate contested meanings" (p. 73). Moon (2004) highlighted the impor-tance of a constructivist view of reflection: by embracing a network of linked ideas, the judgment of meaning in this constructivist view is rela-tive and based on synthesizing new information into existing structures. A constructivist view of reflection allows the learner to determine the mean-ingfulness of something based on their past experiences and multiple identities in the context of the situation (Moon, 2004). Though various theoretical approaches support knowing about reflection, constructivism embraces both individual ways of making meaning as well as the opportu-nity to aggregate context specific information.

Leadership is a socially constructed phenomena (Dugan, 2017). A pos-itivist or technical approach to leadership focuses on universal truths (Dugan, 2017) and potentially would not include reflection. In research, a positivist approach focuses on controlling for the experiences and identi-ties people bring to the leadership process and the contexts in which leadership takes place (Dugan, 2017). A postmodern view of leadership focuses on questioning "truths" and challenging the status quo (Dugan, 2017); in this view, asking questions may be more of the focus than searching for knowledge through reflection. A constructivist view of reflection in leadership learning creates space for understanding that experience, identity, and context impact how learners create knowledge (Dugan, 2017). In this way, a constructivist view of reflection in leadership learning prioritizes individual perspectives and acknowledges subjectivity. Critical reflection in leadership learning draws on the critical theory par-adigm to include an understanding of power and the significance of tak-ing action on the knowledge generated from reflection. Postindustrial leadership theories focus more on the leadership process and are influ-enced by constructivist, critical, and postmodern paradigms (Kezar, Car-ducci, & Contreras-McGavin, 2006; Rosch & Anthony, 2012). Kezar et al. (2006) noted a social constructivist approach to leadership research is well suited to explore meaning making, and it enables researchers to "focus attention on understanding various interpretations of situations to paint more complex pictures than we have had in the past" (p. 20). Our approach to reflection in leadership learning embraces constructivism as a paradigm that aligns with a postindustrial view of leadership and acknowledges the experiences and identities of individuals in context.

LACK OF CLARITY REGARDING REFLECTION

Both reflection and leadership have been critiqued for lacking clarity, and one of the persistent criticisms of reflection is that it is poorly defined (Beauchamp, 2015; Liu, 2015; Rodgers, 2002; Thompson & Pascal, 2012). Speare and Henshall (2014) summarized the challenge that "Reflection is a broad term and may be described as a low consensus concept" (p. 808). Kember, McKay, Sinclair, and Wong Yuet (2008) noted "many write about reflection with the apparent assumption that everyone knows what it is" (p. 369). An aspect with great potential for confusion is when reflection is used as "a noun, a verb, an adjective, a process, and/or an outcome" (Rodgers, 2002, p. 40).

In the survey of reflection in leadership learning, participants were asked to describe reflection. Almost all of the respondents included some element of looking back, and the largest group of responses entailed looking back on past experiences or actions. Another group of responses focused on looking back to analyze, consider improvements, apply information to the future, or assess and evaluate. A third group of responses equated reflection with "engaging in serious thought" or "thinking deeply about an experience, thought or concept." Other responses focused on self-evaluation or introspection. The range of responses indicate students had at least a partial understanding of reflection; most understood the looking back or analysis aspect of reflection while fewer considered how their analysis might apply to the future.

We recognize no definition will be all encompassing or without critique; to not attempt a description for these reasons would be both irresponsible and perpetuate the frustration with using a term that has not been clearly defined. It is also important to recognize that we may collectively spend so long defining reflection, we may fail to acknowledge threats and opportunities for this important pedagogy and render our work irrelevant. Our goal is to elevate reflection beyond thinking (Thompson & Pascal, 2012) without overtheorizing. To that end, our hope is not just to craft a definition. We hope to outline reflection in a way that is broad enough to serve leadership educators, and narrow enough to provide clear guidance for applying reflection in leadership learning.

ELEMENTS OF REFLECTION

Reflection is rooted in philosophy; as an educational concept, reflection developed through multiple pedagogical and disciplinary lenses. Above we described both the challenge of not defining terminology and the significance of a constructivist framework. Given the tension created by these two competing frames of reference, rather than developing a single definition, we outline elements that inform our understanding of reflection in leadership learning. These elements include reflection as a cognitive and affective process; structured activities to facilitate and assess learning; catalyzed by uncertainty or perplexity; ongoing and consistent; and supported by guidance, mentorship, or coaching.

Cognitive and Affective Process

At its core, reflection is a process of thinking and learning. Rogers (2001) noted in a review of definitions of reflection, "all authors clearly stated or at least strongly implied that reflection is a cognitive process or activity" (p. 40–41). Although reflection is about learning, Cranton and Taylor (2012) describe how adult learning theories have shifted over time from a focus on the cognitive process of acquiring knowledge and skills toward a more holistic approach that includes social and embodied learning. Reflection can also focus on the affective dimension. Boud, Keogh, and Walker (1985b) noted, "the reflective process is a complex one in which both feelings and cognition are closely interrelated and interactive" (p. 11). Moon (2004) alleged "emotion is central to reflective processes" and described how emotions can influence knowledge, influence the process of reflection, or arise from the process of reflection. As part of emotionally intelligent leadership, Shankman, Allen, and Haber-Curran (2015) highlighted the importance of reflection for gaining self-awareness of abilities, perceptions, and emotions.

Structured Activities to Facilitate and Assess Learning

In addition to cognitive and affective processes just described, reflection includes structured activities (Hatcher & Bringle, 1997). These structured activities can be used to assess learning (Ash & Clayton, 2009; Guthrie & Jenkins, 2018). Eyler and Giles (1999) described the importance of contextualized reflection which includes both the "style and place for conducting reflection" as well as appropriate methods (p. 184). Although some places may enhance reflection, it is important to acknowl-

edge that some contexts "may be the cause of problems that hinder reflection" because situations or power structures inhibit authentic reflection
(Beauchamp, 2015, p. 129). Eyler, Giles, and Schmeide (1996) organized
reflection activities into categories of reading, writing, doing and telling.
In Chapter 4 we describe reflection as an instructional strategy and a
means for assessing learning; in the companion manual, we provide
guidelines for contemplative, creative, digital, discussion, narrative, and
written reflection activities.

Catalyzed by Uncertainty or Perplexity

Reflection often results from disequilibrium; many works on reflection
highlight the role of challenge, puzzlement, or confusion to prompt
reflection. An influx of new information, as experience or theory, may
prompt learners to consider their actions and beliefs. Dewey (1933) distinguished reflection from thinking by "(1) a state of doubt, hesitation,
perplexity, mental difficulty, in which thinking originates, and (2) an act
of searching, hunting, inquiring, to find material that will resolve the
doubt, settle and dispose of the perplexity" (p. 12). Eyler and Giles (1999)
noted growth was dependent "on puzzlement, on challenge to current
perspectives, and on the challenge to resolve the conflict" (p. 184).
Mezirow (1990) described the role of the "disorienting dilemma"—an
external event or exposure to eye-opening media—which could serve as a
catalyst to reconsider presuppositions and facilitate perspective change.
Rogers (2001) pointed out many reflection frameworks also highlight willingness or readiness as precursors for reflection.

Ongoing and Consistent

Ongoing reflection can refer to regular instances for reflection activities (Eyler, 2001; Hatcher & Bringle, 1997), lifelong learning (Eyler &
Giles, 1999), or an iterative state of reflection (Heifetz & Linsky, 2002).
Eyler (2001) described reflection as occurring before, during, and after
engaged learning. Reflection before an experience can help surface
assumptions or serve as a benchmark; if reflection has been sufficiently
integrated, learners are better positioned to make meaning following
experience than if reflection is not introduced until the end (Eyler, 2001).
Eyler and Giles (1999) noted the significance of continuous reflection:
"learning is never finished but is a lifelong process of understanding" (p.
183). Using the metaphor of the balcony and the dance floor, Heifetz and

Linsky (2002) described reflective thinking in adaptive leadership as a constant and iterative process.

Supported by Guidance, Mentorship, or Coaching

Although reflection may be an individual pursuit, there is broad agreement reflection is supported by others: Rogers (2001) noted most of the reflection frameworks "stressed the importance of education in helping individuals develop habits of reflective thoughts" (p. 46). Sanford's (1967) theory of challenge and support accurately reflects the tension for educators framing reflection for students. Eyler and Giles (1999) described the importance of coaching students through reflection by providing emotional and intellectual support. They also pointed out the significance of interaction and feedback (Eyler & Giles, 1999). In particular, relationships are important for reflection in leadership learning. Dugan and Komives (2007) found mentoring influenced students' potential for socially responsible leadership. Dugan, Kodrama, Correia, and Associates (2013) described how "sociocultural conversations with peers are the single strongest predictor of socially responsible leadership capacity" because as part of these conversations, students have to articulate their perspectives, understand other worldviews, and consider how their values fit into a larger social structure (p. 9). In Chapter 6 we explore the role of reflective leadership educators who play an essential role in supporting and guiding learners through mentorship and coaching.

RELATED TERMINOLOGY

One of the critiques of reflection is confusion over what is meant by this term and how it is applied. Rogers (2001) noted "Confusion regarding terms to describe reflection is even more common in the general press where terms such as self-reflection, reflection, contemplation, introspection, and meditation are sometimes used interchangeably" (p. 40). As we explore reflection, it is important to acknowledge terms that relate or intersect.

Meaning Making

Meaning making is often interchanged with reflection. One of the earlier appearances of meaning making is attributed to Austrian psychiatrist and Holocaust survivor Viktor Frankl. Writing about his time in concentration camps during World War II, Frankl (1946/2006) explored the psychological experiences of prisoners and reflected on the significance of making meaning; he asserted that which was worth living for was meaning, whether in love or in spirituality, and the power for meaning exceeded other drivers. His profound memoir illuminates the significance of meaning making in the face of uncertainty and suffering. Meaning making is also used in constructivism to describe how people interact with the world. Lincoln and Guba (2013) distinguished between physical reality and socially constructed reality. They noted "socially constructed realities, or the meaning-making activities and meaning-ascribed realities" shape responses to the physical environment and social interactions by how people ascribe meaning (Lincoln & Guba, 2013, p. 11).

Postman and Weingartner (1969) critiqued the system of education and proposed strategies for educating learners capable of addressing complex situations. After exploring metaphors for education (lamplighters who illuminate minds, gardeners who cultivate minds, and muscle builders who strengthen minds, among others), they contrasted these conceptualizations of education with meaning making. Meaning making required treating students as unique and acknowledging their identities and ways of knowing to shift the conversation from students confronting objective realities to students at the center of the learning process. Postman and Weingartner (1969) endorsed meaning making for its acknowledgment of the uniqueness of each person's perceptions and the limitlessness of knowing. Although many educational metaphors imply boundaries, "meaning making has no such limitations. There is no end to his educative process. He continues to create new meanings, to make new transactions with his environment" (p. 91). Meaning making is a broad term, and these two examples illustrate the concept in psychology and education, respectively.

Sensemaking

Sensemaking is a process where individuals or groups evaluate information in the context of a socially produced environment (Weick, 1995). Different than understanding or interpreting, sensemaking involves looking at ideas or experiences in retrospect and using contextual cues to understand surroundings. One significant distinction: sensemaking is about understanding something in order to move forward, which means "sufficiency and plausibility take precedence over accuracy" (Weick, 1995, p. 62). Sensemaking in organizations is often prompted by uncertainty or ambiguity: "To deal with ambiguity, interdependent people search for meaning, settle for plausibility, and move on. These are moments of sensemaking" (Weick, Sutcliffe, & Obstfeld, 2005, p. 419). Ng and Tan (2009) highlighted a key difference between sensemaking and reflection: "precisely because of [sensemaking's] significant emphasis on the immediacy of meaning making, reflectivity is low in the agenda" (p. 39). Sensemaking serves an important purpose in organizational theory (Weick et al., 2005), but it may not be the best framework when the focus is enabling paradigm shifts or introducing new ways of thinking in addition to existing meaning structures (Ng & Tan, 2009).

Contemplation

Contemplative pedagogy encompasses a broad range of practices which "all have an inward or first-person focus that creates opportunities for greater connection and insight" and "focus on the present experience, either physical or mental" (Barbezat & Bush, 2014, pp. 5–6). The range of contemplative practices is broad, and the focus is on self-awareness and connecting internal reactions to the world. Through discovering the impact of material on themselves, students are more connected learners. One image that captures many contemplative practices is the tree of contemplative practices from the Center for Contemplative Mind in Society (2014) which includes activities in the categories of stillness, generative, creative, activist, relational, movement, and ritual/cyclical. Focusing specifically on the scholarship of teaching and learning in higher education, Owen-Smith (2018) described contemplative practices as "specific pedagogical exercise that may be integrated in liberal arts courses. They are defined as metacognitive modes and first-person investigations that nurture inner awareness, concentration, insight, and compassion" (p. 24). Instructors can incorporate contemplation into writing or listening activities, and they could also incorporate mindfulness as a contemplative practice to support learning.

Critical Reflection

Critical reflection is both a central concept to understanding reflection in leadership learning *and* one of the more broadly defined, and often contradictory, terms in the literature on reflection. For these reasons, critical reflection warrants its own chapter in this book, and we will explore this in depth in Chapter 5. For now, it is important to acknowledge the term has been used by numerous authors with different underlying meanings, whether referring to reflection that provides critical feedback, promotes critical thinking, is critical for experiential learning, or draws on critical social theory.

EXPERIENTIAL LEARNING

In order to understand experience as part of transformative learning, MacKeracher (2012) sought to define "experience." Broadly, experience is "everything that happens to you between birth and death" which once passed may be retained as memory (MacKeracher, 2012, p. 343). Experience can also include things in which we are not directly involved—the types of political, cultural, and social events that are defining for generations—but which influence behaviors, values, beliefs, or expectations (MacKeracher, 2012). Together, we can understand experience as the interplay of our personal experiences, or subjective knowledge, and culturally imposed experience, or received knowledge (Belenky, Clinchy, Goldberger, & Tarule, 1986); at the intersection of these, particularly when they are in contrast, experience can lead to learning. Experience often refers to opportunities that educators develop for students to achieve learning goals; we must also acknowledge the influence of life experiences that have preceded or are concurrent with curricular and cocurricular learning and are also influential for students.

Experiential learning invites people to engage the world as active participants rather than passive observers. Experiential learning is anchored in the work of Dewey (1933) who implored educators to shift away from rote memorization. Freire (1970) rejected what he called the banking concept of education: the type of education "with the teacher as narrator" whereby students "memorize mechanically" (pp. 52–53). He lamented, "it turns them into 'containers,' into 'receptacles' to be 'filled' by the teacher" (Freire, 1970, p. 53). Similarly, Moon (2004) distinguished the brick wall view of learning, where teachers provide knowledge that builds up a structure, from a constructivist view of learning where learning is accumulated and assimilated into "a vast but flexible network of ideas and feelings" (pp. 16–17). These perspectives on learning, which shift the focus from instructors to learners, invite opportunities for experiential learning. As we will see in Chapter 3, learner-centered leadership education is significant in order to redirect the focus from activities or programs to the outcomes of leadership learning.

Narrowly defined, leadership education includes the collection of learning activities and educational environments intended to foster and enhance leadership abilities (Brungardt, 1996); pragmatically, leadership education is the practice of facilitating leadership learning to build human capacity. Informed by leadership theory and research, leadership education takes place in both curricular and cocurricular educational contexts (Andenoro et al., 2013). Guthrie and Jenkins (2018) asserted, "leadership educators should look to experiential learning theories to ground leadership learning" (p. 108). Leadership education often employs active and experiential pedagogies, such as service-learning, discussion, case studies, team-based learning, self-and peer-assessment, role play, simulation, games, and art to engage students in learning about both leadership and leader identity development (Guthrie & Jenkins, 2018). Experience is embedded in the grounding elements of the reflection in leadership learning framework. Students may be able to develop a theoretical knowledge of leadership through passive means; to develop knowledge, skills, and values that enable leadership development and leader identity development, students must have opportunities for active learning including problem-solving, relationship building, and active engagement in the world.

Active and engaged learning is a powerful tool; however, Ash and Clayton (2009) were clear "experience alone can be a problematic teacher" (p. 25). Without reflection, "experiential learning can all too easily allow students to reinforce stereotypes... students may leave applied learning experiences with little capacity to turn learning into improved action" (Ash & Clayton, 2009, p. 26). Jacoby (2015) echoed these dangers: "experience without critical reflection ... can all too easily allow students to reinforce their stereotypes about people who are different from themselves, develop simplistic solutions to complex problems, and generalize inaccurately based on limited data" (p. 26). Educators utilizing experiential learning must include reflection to challenge students to think deeply and avoid reinforcing stereotypes or allowing partial information to substitute for a complete picture. As an experiential pedagogy, leadership education requires reflection. In Chapter 4, we will explore instructional and assessment strategies for reflection in leadership learning.

PEDAGOGICAL AND DISCIPLINARY APPLICATIONS

Although experiential learning and reflection span disciplines, there is a significant concentration of literature about reflection related to service-learning and community engagement, as well as in the fields of nursing, teacher education, and social work. These disciplines potentially focus on reflection because they often include practicum, field experience, student teaching, internship, or other in-depth periods of engagement during which students reflect on experience. These disciplines consistently engage students in interactions with individuals from diverse backgrounds; in Chapter 3 we discuss the role of identity in leadership development, and in Chapter 5 we discuss how critical reflection supports leadership learning and engagement in broader social contexts.

Service-Learning and Community Engagement

A significant portion of the literature on reflection is concentrated in the pedagogy of service-learning. With the expansion of service-learning in the mid-1990s came several seminal publications focused on the role of reflection in experiential learning and facilitating reflection including Eyler and Giles (1999), Hatcher and Bringle (1997), and Eyler et al. (1996), among others. As service-learning has continued, and practitioners have debated the definition and execution of the pedagogy, there have been attendant conversations about reflection and its role in service-learning. Reflection has been called the hyphen between service and learning (Eyler, 2001; Jacoby, 2015). Service-learning practitioners and scholars have focused on the role of reflection before, during, and after service (Eyler & Giles, 1999) as well as the importance of anchoring reflection in learning outcomes (Ash & Clayton, 2009). Scholars and practitioners continue to advance scholarship and practice on reflection in service-learning; for example, recent work has focused on community members as part of the reflection process (d'Arlach, Sanchez, Feuer, 2009), engaging students in critical reflection for social justice (Mitchell, 2008; Owen, 2016), the long-term impact of reflection as part of community engagement programs (Mitchell et al., 2015), and faculty reflection on approaches to service-learning (Miller-Young et al., 2015).

Nursing

Reflective learning has a long history in nursing. Beginning in Australia in the 1980s, reflection was a key strategy for incorporating experiential and active learning into nursing classrooms (Taylor, Freshwater, Sherwood, & Estherhuizen, 2008). Horton-Deutsch and Sherwood (2008) noted an "emphasis on developing self-awareness as a leadership strategy has contributed to the global spread of reflection in nursing education, practice and research" (p. 946). Reflection is key for helping nurses transition to a fast-paced and complex work environment. Some of the benefits of reflective learning for nurses include evaluating underlying beliefs and values, developing confidence in choosing interventions, and becoming emotionally competent (Horton-Deutsch & Sherwood, 2008). To support skill development, critical thinking, and affective learning, nurse educators have used journaling and assessed students' level of reflective practice (Chirema, 2007; Garrity, 2013; Thorpe, 2004). Digital storytelling has been used with nursing students to promote affective learning and skill development (Price, Strodtman, Brough, Lonn, & Luo, 2015; LeBlanc, 2017). It is important to note nurse educators have also critiqued reflective practice (Burton, 2000; Cotton, 2001; Hannigan, 2001).

Teacher Education

Another discipline steeped in reflection is teacher education. Two themes emerged in teacher education literature on reflection: establishing criteria for evaluating reflective thought and engaging preservice teachers in critical reflection. Hatton and Smith (1995) are often cited for their research which developed criteria to determine levels of reflection from written reflections completed by students in a teacher education program. Ward and McCotter (2004) argued reflection risked being subsumed by the standards movement, wondering "Is reflection nothing more than a tool for helping teachers increase student test scores or is there value in reflection on broader themes such as social justice?" (p. 244). Using a grounded theory approach, they developed a rubric to support scaffolding of reflection for preservice teachers (Ward & McCotter, 2004). Brookfield's (2017) *Becoming a Critically Reflective Teacher* has been influential in education and beyond. One of the persistent questions raised in the literature relates to the capacity for developing critical reflection, and the publications that address this question are too numerous to list. Similar to nursing, there have been challenges to the application of reflection in teacher education. (Beauchamp, 2015).

Social Work

Similarly, social work incorporates significant reflection in preparation programs and practice (Gould & Taylor, 1996; Thompson & Thompson, 2008). In an interprofessional approach, White, Fook, and Gardner (2006) edited a text that explored *Critical Reflection in Health and Social Care* in order to provide "practitioners, educators and researchers in health and welfare with concepts and methods to help them to 'see what they do not see'" (p. xii). Developing a reflective practice may be particularly useful for professionals as they encounter a range of diverse people in their work (Frost, 2010). Furman, Coyne, and Negi (2008) used written narratives and poetry to facilitate reflection for social work students participating in an international experience. Walmsley and Birkbeck (2006) used personal narratives to help students reflect on their values and the influence of values in the social work profession. Chaumba (2015) found students in a human behavior course who used blogs to reflect on field experiences increased their level of reflective thinking. As in other fields, there is concern that having students reflect on challenging and personal topics might invoke resistance, especially when the reflections are part of a graded assignment (Newcomb, Burton, & Edwards, 2018).

REFLECTION MODELS

There are a number of models for reflection on experiential learning: promoting reflection in learning (Boud, Kough, & Walker, 1985a); DEAL (Describe, Examine, and Articulate Learning) model (Ash & Clayton, 2009); and meaning, internalization, and externalization (Le Cornu, 2009), to name a few. These models operationalize reflection and provide a framework for educators to engage learners in the process of reflection. One of the most popular models for reflection is the "What? So What? Now What?" model which is deceptively simple while providing a solid anchor for reflective practice.

In the literature, there are two texts that reference the origin of the "What? So What? Now What?" model of reflection. One posits the model was adapted from Kolb's cycle of experiential learning (1984) by the Campus Opportunity Outreach League in 1995 (Ash & Clayton, 2004). The other says Rolfe, Freshwater, and Jasper (2001) adapted the model from Borton's (1970) *Reach, Touch, and Teach: Student Concerns and Process Education*. In many cases, this model is not cited at all as the use has become so ubiquitous. Having two origin stories for this model illustrates the challenge in tracing the progression of thinking and scholarship as it relates to reflection; regardless of the origin, the "What? So What? Now What?" model is used broadly in reflection. The simplicity makes it useful for engaging learners at all points in their experience, but it also belies the potential complexity that comes from repeated cycles through these questions.

The first question—"What?"—focuses primarily on occurrences. The purpose is to look at what happened and describe events before interpreting meaning. The second question—"So what?"—explores significance and shifts from description to interpretation. This question focuses on responses, reactions, and feelings with a focus on evaluation. The final question—"Now what?"—moves from lessons learned toward application. This question focuses on implications and application to the future. Although the questions are simple and broadly applicable, they are also adaptable and offer the opportunity to scaffold learning with increasing cognitive complexity. Many reflection models map to these essential questions making this a useful entry level model and a grounding frame for more complex reflection.

METHODS FOR REFLECTION

In the reflection in leadership learning framework, one of the grounding elements is exposure to reflective practice. It is critical for educators to understand the philosophy that underscores reflection and to instill in students some of the rich information that substantiates reflection as a tool for teaching and learning. Simultaneously, students need exposure to reflection methods and activities. For example, if students perceive reflection as writing in a journal, which is often what comes to mind when people hear reflection, they may avoid the practice because they are averse to journaling. However, knowing there are a multitude of methods for processing experiences may help engage students in learning. In the simplest form, reflection can consist of writing or engaging in discussion with another person; neither enterprise requires extensive tools nor training. However, there are numerous activities and prompts that can support a rich reflective practice. These methods can be sequenced to help learners achieve greater depth of understanding or engage a breadth of ideas.

FROM THEORY TO PRACTICE

Reflection is a rich and complex concept with a deep philosophical grounding. In tracing the development of reflection, we have described the diffusion among disciplines and described concepts related to reflection. The elements of reflection outlined here will be connected to the leadership learning framework (Guthrie & Jenkins, 2018) in Chapter 3. Leadership education is well poised among disciplines to advance the conversation about reflection. As an interdisciplinary and multidisciplinary field that employs experiential pedagogies, leadership educators include reflection throughout curricular and cocurricular experiences. As leadership learning is focused on relationships that sustain change, reflection on leadership learning has the potential to enhance the capacity of students to engage meaningfully with others and facilitate a change process. A shift away from reflection on the individual level toward reflection that influences professional practice would bring reflection more in line with its progressive foundations and enhance the power of this practice for student learning as well as for graduates and professionals (Kilminster et al., 2010). For reflection to reclaim a role as a transformative pedagogy, leadership educators should focus on reflection as a philosophy, a method, and an outcome. In this way, students who learn about leadership can learn from reflection and also apply reflection to their leadership practice. As lifelong reflective learners, students will be better equipped to learn as individuals, evaluate their work in context, and advance conversations about broader societal issues based on the insights gained from reflection.

CHAPTER 3

FRAMING LEADERSHIP LEARNING

As seen in the previous chapter, reflection is challenging to define, and leadership is no different. Interestingly, when concepts are difficult to define, scholars, educators, and practitioners can become preoccupied with creating a definition. In some cases, it becomes nearly impossible to agree on one as a field and people may feel unable to move forward. On the other hand, by not defining terms such as reflection and leadership, the concepts become so broad that scholars, educators, and practitioners include overreaching definitions which can dilute their potency. In this chapter, we will define leadership in order to situate our conversation of reflection in leadership and leadership learning. Then, we will discuss leadership learning and how we can understand pedagogy and learning assessment related to leadership learning.

Historically, institutions of higher education have prioritized leadership as part of their mission statements (Dugan & Komives, 2007; Zimmerman-Oster & Burkhardt, 1999), however Guthrie and Osteen (2016) called attention to the necessity of higher education to reclaim its purpose in leadership development. One means of accomplishing this is to seek new ways of providing leadership learning opportunities for all students. Integrating reflection and leadership learning is a powerful way to broaden and deepen leadership learning.

DEFINING LEADERSHIP

For the past several centuries, global societies have expressed interest in developing leaders (Ayman, Adams, Fisher, & Hartman, 2003). Leadership

Thinking to Transform: Reflection in Leadership Learning
pp. 45–61
Copyright © 2019 by Information Age Publishing
All rights of reproduction in any form reserved.

and developing leaders are not new topics; some argue all modern education, including leadership, evolved from the teachings of Plato and Aristotle (Birkelund, 2000). By mentoring and teaching Alexander the Great, Aristotle demonstrated the importance of educating future leaders (Burkhardt & Zimmerman-Oster, 1999). This historical snapshot provides context for the foundation and evolution of leadership as well as the interdisciplinary and multidisciplinary nature of leadership.

Over time, the definition of leadership has been more debated than agreed upon (Guthrie & Jenkins, 2018) as evidenced by the variability in leadership theories and models. Kellerman (2012) found over 1,500 definitions and 40 models of leadership. Individuals may perceive leadership differently based on their identities, experiences, and worldviews, which makes defining leadership complex. As discussed in Chapter 2, both reflection and leadership are socially constructed; to apply this to leadership means "Leadership does not functionally exist. It represents an abstract set of concepts derived by people to explain and make meaning of observations from the world" (Dugan, 2017, p. 8). As a social construct, leadership holds different meanings for different people (Guthrie, Bertrand Jones, Osteen, & Hu, 2013).

Burns (1978) is credited as the first person to confront traditional Western leadership scholars by challenging the notion of a leader as one individual creating and executing a vision. In 1993, Rost (1993) moved Burns' (1978) work on the conceptualization of leadership from an industrial to a postindustrial model. Industrial models associate leadership with position, title, being at the top of power hierarchies, and directing others, or, as Rost (1993) summarized, simply good management. Postindustrial conceptions of leadership are rooted in reciprocal relationships essential to the leadership process (Rost, 1993). The postindustrial leadership paradigm differentiates leader the person, from leadership, the process.

In our survey of reflection in leadership learning, students were asked how they define leadership. The responses demonstrated a range of thought processes that included both industrial ("Someone who takes charge and a person that other people follow") and postindustrial ("Leadership is not a position or a title, it is an action and example") approaches to leadership. Some of the patterns that emerged were leadership as working toward a common goal, taking charge of a situation or a group, setting an example, and influencing other people. Although some students who completed the survey had experience with curricular or cocurricular leadership programs, other students may not have engaged in leadership learning. This range of responses demonstrates a continued need for leadership learning in higher education.

The foundational belief that regardless of positional power anyone may engage in the leadership process aligns with higher education's goal of advancing all students' leadership (Guthrie & Jenkins, 2018). There is a clear distinction between leader and leadership: "*Leaders* are the individuals, with or without formal positions of authority, who work collectively to tackle social problems. *Leadership* is the collaboration of these leaders, interactions between leaders and followers, and the process occurring among and between them" (Guthrie & Jenkins, 2018, p. 5, emphasis added). Reflection is required at every point of a leader's development and the process of leadership in which they are engaging.

REFLECTION AND LEADERSHIP

Reflection is a distinguishing factor between industrial and postindustrial approaches to leadership. Holding a prominent role or title, having a position at the top of a hierarchy, or managing others may be achieved without significant reflection. Arguably, reflection is required to understand systems and work collaboratively with others for a common purpose. The relational component of postindustrial leadership requires reflection on self and relationships with others. Reflection supports the development of the person, or the leader, and facilitates the process of leadership. In the opening chapter, we introduced the reflection in leadership learning framework. This framework does not describe a process for reflection, but rather it anchors the reflection process in leadership learning. The grounding elements set the stage for broad and deep reflection by preparing learners for engagement with experiences and ideas. The support structures outline possibilities for leadership educators to support students and facilitate reflection with students in curricular and cocurricular settings. The outcomes of the framework describe possibilities for enhanced leadership beliefs and actions that result from learning about leadership and practicing reflection. This framework supports the central role of reflection in leadership learning and provides a guide for learners and educators for enhancing reflection as an iterative and complex process.

Chapter 1 referenced a few leadership models that include elements of reflection: social change model of leadership development (Higher Education Research Institute, 1996), adaptive leadership (Heifetz & Linsky, 2002), leadership identity development model (Komives, Longerbeam, Owen, Mainella, & Osteen, 2006), emotionally intelligent leadership (Shankman, Allen, & Haber-Curran, 2015) and culturally relevant leadership learning model (Bertrand Jones, Guthrie, & Osteen, 2016). All of these models include elements of reflection for self-development and enhancing relationships within groups and communities. Two additional leadership models that highlight the significance of reflection for leaders and leadership development are authentic leadership (Avolio & Gardner, 2005) and conviction in action (Roberts, 2007).

Authentic leadership is defined as an intra- and interpersonal process that considers an individual's capacity to learn and lead from a grounded sense of self (Northouse, 2016). This sense of self stems from self-aware-ness, relational transparency, internalized moral perspective, and bal-anced processing, which come from intense self-reflection (Avolio & Gardner, 2005; Walumbwa, Avolio, Gardner, Wernsing, & Peterson, 2008). The focus on interaction between leaders and followers connects authen-tic leadership to leadership development. This interaction reinforces and mutually develops leaders and followers' authentic capacity (Guthrie et al., 2013).

Robert's (2007) definition of leadership as "conviction in action" is both beautifully simple and deeply complex (p. 96). Conviction in action principles are grounded in presence or one's ability to be aware of and attuned to possibilities that exist outside of the self (Roberts, 2007). Though not synonymous with reflection, contemplative practices includ-ing mindfulness serve as a complement for reflection and enhance one's ability to be present. Conviction in action focuses primarily on developing ways of being including honesty, openness, and courage which may be developed through reflection and self-awareness. By becoming more aware of themselves, students may also become more aware of others. Awareness of others is foundational for teaching students about the pow-erful tension in leading: "it is all about you (leader) and it is not about you at all (leadership)—all at the same time" (Guthrie et al., 2013, p. 19). It is important for leadership educators to provide opportunities for students to not only learn about leadership but to understand this tension. One way this can be accomplished is through reflection on the process of lead-ership.

LEARNER-CENTERED LEADERSHIP EDUCATION

Merriam, Caffarella, and Baumgartner (2007) focused on learning as "a personal process—but a process that is shaped by the context of adult life and the society in which one lives" (p. 1). Learning is a process that can take place in many formal and informal environments (Merriam et al., 2007); how a person defines learning is reflective of their philosophical orientation. We have described the constructivist nature of both reflection and leadership. Merriam et al. (2007) described learning from a construc-tivist frame as "learners construct their own knowledge from their experi-ences. The cognitive process of meaning-making is emphasized as both an individual mental activity and a socially interactive interchange" (p. 297). Mezirow's (2012) description is similar: learning is "the process of using a prior interpretation to construe a new or revised interpretation of the meaning of one's experience as a guide to future action" (p. 74). Reflection is central to both descriptions of learning. Leadership is a process of learning that requires individuals to reflect on and learn from experiences. Through reflection on leadership experiences, individuals seek to discover their leader identities while working collaboratively in communities of practice (Antonacopoulou & Bento, 2004). For the purposes of this text, we use Guthrie and Jenkins (2018) definition of leadership learning as "changes in knowledge, skills, behavior, attitudes, and values resulting from educational experiences, both curricular and cocurricular in nature, associated with the activity of leadership" (p. 57). Focusing on leadership learning as an outcome "opens the conversation for a more complex, thoughtful, and intentional approach to the design of educational opportunities" (Guthrie & Jenkins, 2018, p. 57).

Mission statements for institutions of higher education have increasingly focused on developing future leaders (Chunoo & Osteen, 2016). This requires realigning the purpose and context of postsecondary education with leadership learning, and better preparing educators to provide leadership learning opportunities. The first step is reframing leadership education to focus on leadership learning in order to develop both curricular and cocurricular leadership programs. Guthrie and Jenkins (2018) synthesized critiques of leadership programs, pointing out "leadership development programs are often created from a buffet of activities educators experienced themselves or observed while working with other students" which results in programs "filled with entertaining activities generated around the availability of facilitators ... void of any sense of content or curricular sequencing" (p. 55). In the absence of structured content or learning outcomes, it would be challenging to incorporate meaningful reflection or to expect assessable learning gains. Postsecondary education should focus on learning; when learning, not instruction, is at the core of education, student- and learning-centered approaches emerge (Barr & Tagg, 1995). A learner-centered focus places educators as conduits of knowledge rather than merely distributors (Guthrie & Jenkins, 2018). Shifting from an education focus to learner centricity is essential for creating intentional and holistic leadership programs.

The distinction between leadership development and leader identity development is significant for defining leadership. To clarify, "*leader* development focuses on individual students' capacity and identity, with or without formal authority, to engage in the leadership process ... [and] ... leader*ship* development is a collective focus on a group's relationships and process" (Guthrie et al., 2013, p. 15, emphasis in original). With this distinction in mind, we can understand leadership learning as a dynamic process where individuals both influence and are influenced by experiences. Reflection is critical for experiences to have educational value. As described in chapter 1, having an experience is insufficient for learning; learning takes place when students consider an experience in the context of their previous beliefs and assumptions in order to evaluate their thoughts, actions, and beliefs going forward. When we focus on leadership learning as the outcome, rather than the content provided, we can design thoughtful, purposeful, and reflective leadership education programs that help students make meaning of developmental experiences.

LEADERSHIP LEARNING FRAMEWORK

For almost 3 decades, the training, education, and development model (Roberts & Ullom, 1989) has served as a guide for leadership educators. In 2012, Guthrie and Osteen expanded the training, education, and development model to include engagement as a critical element for learning leadership. Although the concepts of training, education, and development seem straightforward, leadership learning literature has used this terminology inconsistently (Sowcik & Allen, 2013) and terms such as leadership education, leadership studies, leadership training, and leadership development are often used interchangeably. Although these terms are often used to stand in for one another (Ayman, Adams, Fisher, & Hartman, 2003), each is distinct in its application and implications for leadership learning.

Guthrie and Jenkins (2018) introduced the leadership learning framework which "leadership educators can use theoretically, conceptually, and in practice to create programs that intentionally connect pedagogy with learning outcomes" (p. 56). The leadership learning framework shown in Figure 3.1 (Guthrie & Jenkins, 2018) expands the training, education, and development model (Roberts & Ullom, 1989) as a way to approach leadership learning, builds on previous work in this area, and delves into literature from various disciplines to propose six aspects of leadership learning. These six aspects of leadership learning include knowledge, development, training, observation, engagement, and metacognition. The leadership learning framework (Guthrie & Jenkins, 2018) is a tool educators can use to better understand the multiple ways in which students learn and create programs that are learner centered. Using the metaphor of a steering wheel, the leadership learning framework (Guthrie & Jenkins, 2018) offers a mechanism for students and creates accountability for them to direct their own learning.

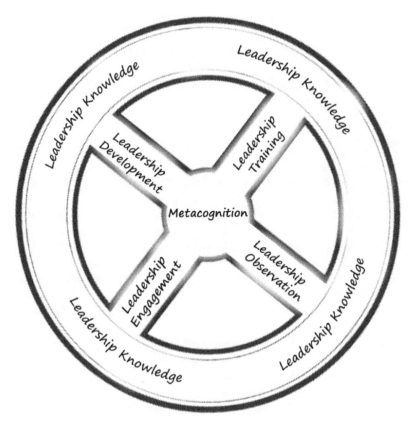

Figure 3.1.   Leadership learning framework. Reprinted from Guthrie and Jenkins (2018).

In the leadership learning framework (Guthrie & Jenkins, 2018), leadership knowledge encompasses the whole wheel. Guthrie and Jenkins (2018) highlighted the ubiquity of leadership knowledge: "leadership knowledge acquisition occurs in all programs, even if only by using language about leadership that may not have been used previously" (p. 57). Knowledge of leadership language, concepts, skills, and theories is connected to all aspects of the framework and is foundational for leadership learning. The importance of leadership knowledge underscores the significance of language and how learning the language of leadership begins with acquiring leadership knowledge. This is also echoed by the reflection in leadership learning framework where leadership theory is a grounding element; knowledge of leadership theory provides a base to which students can anchor or compare experiential learning. Working in from the outer perimeter of the framework of leadership knowledge, the four aspects of development, training, observation, and engagement all connect to meta-cognition. Guthrie and Jenkins (2018) centered metacognition as a synthesis of critical thought essential to making meaning of and applying learning. As we describe each of the elements of the leadership learning framework, we describe the role of reflection for each component.

Leadership Knowledge

To acquire leadership knowledge is to obtain information and insights about the process of leadership. Allen and Shehane (2016) described this cognitive process as declarative where information is often presented in a formal setting by an expert; the emphasis is on acquiring information and mental processing. A vital part of leadership education is learning leadership theories, concepts, and language. Developing a leadership program begins with identifying what knowledge students should learn: "the 'necessary' knowledge … falls into two broad categories: technical knowledge of the expertise and skills deemed requisite to leadership either generally or in particular areas and humanistic knowledge about people, both as individuals and as members of groups" (Harvey & Jenkins, 2014, p. 77). It is important to note gaining leadership knowledge transcends classroom experiences; knowledge can be acquired in curricular or cocurricular settings and through the lens of a leader or a follower. Although a class provides structure through established learning outcomes and assessment, leadership learning in cocurricular contexts is critical for holistic learning. Outcome-based knowledge assessment takes place at a specific experience or event, which can extend beyond a traditional classroom setting (Bresciani, Gardner, & Hickmott, 2012).

As students are exposed to leadership knowledge, an infusion of new and potentially conflicting ideas may prompt reflection. This resonates with the grounding idea of leadership theory in the reflection in leadership learning framework: students who hold an industrial view of leadership and are exposed to postindustrial theories and models may be challenged to reconsider their beliefs and actions in light of new information. Having a foundation of leadership knowledge allows students to make connections and comparisons between experiences and the theories, concepts, and language of leadership learning. In the purest form, leadership knowledge comes to life through praxis. Freire (1970/1996) described praxis as action and reflection, stimulated by dialogue, to transform the world. Buschlen and Guthrie (2014) described how students in leadership programs can develop leadership knowledge by applying theories and concepts to personal experiences; the practical application of theory and reflection demonstrated through action completes a praxis model.

Leadership Development

Leadership development focuses on the intrapersonal and human aspects of leadership learning (Guthrie & Jenkins, 2018). Nadler (1984) noted the emphasis on personal growth distinguished development from training or education, and he offered a future-oriented and person-centered definition of development: "learning for growth of the individual but not related to a specific present or future job" (p. 22). Guthrie and Osteen (2012) synthesized these concepts and added leadership engagement—the application and practice of leadership skills (from training), knowledge (from education), and values (from development) to solve problems or change conditions—demonstrating the interconnections between aspects of leadership learning.

Allen and Shehane (2016) highlighted the potential for growth through leadership development, which is "characterized by new insights and progression, can include an individual's motivations, values, identity, emotions, and potential in relation to the activity of leadership" (p. 43). Learning in this area is concentrated on the individual including their identity (Day, Harrison, & Halpin, 2009; Guthrie et al., 2013), personal motivation and readiness to lead (Avolio & Hannah, 2008), values and needs (Maslow, 1970), and multiple other dimensions of self (Allen & Shehane, 2016). Leadership development encompasses knowing about and having experience with many of the elements of emotionally intelligent leadership (Shankman et al., 2015) including "ethics, consciousness of self, authenticity, citizenship, receiving feedback, engaging in reflection, healthy self-esteem, flexibility, and emotional self-regulation" (Guthrie & Jenkins, 2018, p. 61). When we describe leadership development, we also include leader development. Leadership development emphasizes relationships as well as opportunities to integrate with and understand groups while leader development focuses on the individual, including intrapersonal growth and the opportunity to understand self (Day, 2000).

Many of the instructional and assessment strategies Guthrie and Jenkins (2018) identified for leadership development lend themselves to reflection including: personal mission statements, values-based videos, vision boards, mind mapping, and storytelling. Additionally, there are several self-assessment tools leadership educators may use to facilitate self-exploration and leadership development (Guthrie & Jenkins, 2018). These reflection activities, among others, provide opportunities for students to become aware of their multiple and intersecting identities (Guthrie et al., 2013), clarify their values (Fritz & Guthrie, 2017), engage in affective learning (Mahoney, 2017), and develop empathy in order to connect with others (Shankman et al., 2015). Understanding identity, values, and emotions prepares students to achieve the outcomes in the reflection in leadership learning framework such as developing self-awareness and navigating relationships and change processes. Reflection supports students through developing a leader identity and preparing for the leadership process.

Leadership Training

Leadership training is focused on the skill- and competency-based behavioral aspects of leadership learning. This type of learning requires scaffolding so students can practice and build upon lessons toward mastery and assessable changes in behavior. Specifically, leadership training is the space where students show "proficiency in demonstrating specific tasks associated with the activity of leadership" (Allen & Shehane, 2016, p. 43). In other words, leadership training focuses specifically on what leadership learners are able to do as a result of leadership programs. This aligns with Nadler's (1984) definition of training as "learning related to the present job" (p. 18), which emphasized improved performance on specific tasks. Cocurricular leadership learning programs use leadership training most often (Guthrie & Jenkins, 2018).

When combined with a disciplinary focus, leadership training is well positioned to develop students in meaningful ways within their field of study. Nandan and London (2013) examined graduate programs designed to prepare individuals as global leaders and change agents; they argued leadership training must include opportunities to sharpen interdisciplinary competencies in order to prepare leaders to deal with complex challenges. Implementing interdisciplinary education models in order to teach competencies is vital to comprehensive leadership training efforts. In Chapter 2, we described elements of reflection including how learners can develop skills related to reflection. Reflection may be a means to achieve learning outcomes, but learning about reflection and practicing reflection can also be outcomes. Leadership training should include opportunities to reflect on the development of competencies and skills, and, depending upon the context, could also include developing a reflective practice as a skill or identifying reflection as a skill and competency.

Leadership Observation

Leadership observation "refers to the social, cultural, and observational aspects of leadership learning" (Guthrie & Jenkins, 2018, p. 65). Leadership observation focuses on how the learner makes meaning from perceiving how leaders and followers act. As an observer, the learner is a passive recipient of information and not actively engaged in interactions.

Learning influences and is influenced by sociocultural context (Merriam et al., 2007), and through the social learning orientation, context and culture are key to learning (Bandura, 1977). Whether observing several individuals in a collectivist society or a specific leader in another culture, observing others is essential for learning. Mitra (2011) affirmed, "The ways of observing (or looking with intentionality) require us to go another step (or two) and to use our judgment and inference-making abilities to arrive at something resembling knowledge" (p. 185). Looking with intention provides leaders with not only knowledge but also practice in reading environments accurately.

Between the volume of information vying for our attention and the complex situations we deal with daily, it can be difficult to discern patterns; it is critical to be able to see clearly, not only to learn leadership, but also to provide effective leadership. Leadership observation is a passive means of taking in information, and reflection is important for learners to understand and make meaning of what they observe. Experiential educators found having limited exposure to a community or setting can reinforce stereotypes (Ash & Clayton, 2009; Jacoby, 2015). Learners need guiding questions, and sometimes redirection, in order to process observations, particularly in new places or unfamiliar cultural contexts. In order for students to achieve the outcomes in the reflection in leadership learning framework, they must be able to observe situations and use reflection to discern patterns of interaction that inform their knowledge and actions.

Leadership Engagement

Astin (1984) highlighted the importance of engagement and the benefits of student involvement on college campuses. Leadership engagement "refers to the experiential, relational, interactional, and interpersonal aspects of leadership learning" where the learner is an active participant (Guthrie & Jenkins, 2018, p. 67). Learners construct meaning as a result of personal and direct encounters with leadership activities. Allen and Shehane (2016) described the purpose of an experiential and applied dimension of leadership learning: "to provide the learner with new experiences, and the role of the educator is often to help individuals capture and make sense of planned or naturalistic experiences (constructivism) following an activity" (p. 44). Leadership engagement has both behavioral and cognitive dimensions (Trowler, 2013), and favorable outcomes improve when institutions support engagement for leadership learning. Krauss and Hamid (2015) discussed how learning from an engagement perspective is effective for learners globally, not just in the highly researched Western context.

Eyler (2001) said, "Reflection is the hyphen between service-learning" (p. 35); the same idea applies to other experiential learning opportunities, including leadership. Reflection is a critical connector between leadership engagement and learning. Leadership engagement features prominently in the reflection in leadership learning framework as both a grounding element (experiences of leadership engagement) and a support structure (engagement with others to facilitate making meaning of engagement experiences). Additionally, the outcomes in the framework result from engagement and reflection. Leadership engagement supports the development of students and enhances leadership learning (Guthrie & Jenkins, 2018).

Leadership Metacognition

According to Guthrie and Jenkins (2018), leadership metacognition is "the reflective, organizational, systemic, analytical, mindful, evaluative, adaptive, processual, and complex aspect of leadership learning" (p. 69). In this aspect of the framework, the learner is aware of their thought processes about leadership and leadership learning. Flavell (1976) coined the term metacognition and defined it as "one's knowledge concerning one's own cognitive processes and products or anything related to them" (p. 232); this is often paraphrased as "thinking about one's thinking" (Silver, 2013, p. 9). Flavell (1976) offered the following example of metacognitive thought:

> I am engaging in metacognition ... if I notice that I am having more trouble learning A than B; if it strikes me that I should double check C before accepting it as fact; if it occurs to me that I had better scrutinize each and every alternative in any multiple-choice type task situation before deciding which is the best one; if I become aware that I am not sure what the experimenter really wants me to do; if I sense I had better make note of D because I may forget it; if I think to ask someone about E to see if I have it right. Such examples could be multiplied endlessly. (p. 232)

Rooted in psychology (Flavell, 1976) and a cognitivist orientation to learning (Merriam et al., 2007), metacognition contributes to reflection. As part of a model for critical thinking instruction, Halpern (2014) described metacognition as the "executive or 'boss' function that guides how adults use different learning strategies and make decisions about the allocation of limited cognitive resources" (p. 27). In a taxonomy of critical thinking skills, Davies and Barnett (2015) included metacognition at the highest level, along with self-regulation. Silver (2013) highlighted the link between reflection and metacognition: "it is the attention to go *how* one learns that gives rise to the moment of *reflexivity* in reflection and the moment of *meta* in metacognition" and these moments enable learners to step back and review their mental processes (p. 1). By engaging in leadership metacognition, learners can self-assess their process. Metacognitive strategies support both critical thinking and reflection.

Context is significant for leadership learning, and this includes knowing when, where, and why to use particular approaches for learning leadership. Connecting the leadership learning framework to contexts where students from diverse backgrounds can learn leadership is key for students' success. Identity (Jones, 2016), capacity, and efficacy (Dugan, 2017) are critical to the intentional creation of culturally relevant leadership learning opportunities. To explore these concepts, we discuss Bertrand Jones et al.'s (2016) culturally relevant leadership learning model.

CULTURALLY RELEVANT LEADERSHIP LEARNING

The culturally relevant leadership learning model (Bertrand Jones et al., 2016) challenges previous leadership learning paradigms and provides a means for "transforming leadership programs to address the advantages and disadvantages difference creates" (p. 10). As seen in Figure 3.2, the culturally relevant leadership learning model considers learning environments by focusing on contextual dimensions and broader environmental factors. This model recognizes educators' power to influence students' identity, capacity, and efficacy through institutional culture and climate. Mahoney (2017) noted, "The culturally relevant leadership learning model contends that leadership content (what we teach) and pedagogy (how we teach) must align in a supplementary fashion and foster a critical consciousness toward social change" (p. 57). In this way, he said, "Culturally relevant leadership learning harnesses diverse and often-overlooked leadership thought and practice to enhance all students' identity, capacity, and efficacy in leadership development for social change" (Mahoney, 2017, p. 57). The culturally relevant leadership learning model recognizes the power inherent in leadership and relies on intersectional frameworks of identity development (Guthrie et al., 2013; Jones, 2016; Ostick & Wall, 2011) to create learning environments where everyone can engage in the leadership learning process.

Bertrand Jones et al. (2016) grounded culturally relevant leadership learning in two important and foundational areas: culturally relevant pedagogy (Ladson-Billings, 2014) and campus climate (Hurtado, Milem, Clayton-Pederson, & Allen, 1999; Milem, Chang, & Antonio, 2005). Iden-

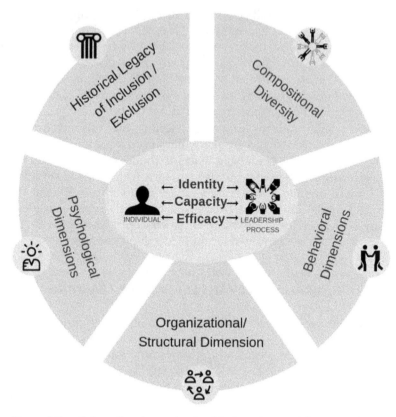

Figure 3.2.   Culturally relevant leadership learning model. Adapted from Bertrand Jones et al. (2016, p. 19).

tity, capacity, and efficacy are at the center for culturally relevant leadership learning. We explore these concepts in the context of developing leadership learning opportunities. Together, identity, capacity, and efficacy describe "a student's way of understanding self as an agent of change through interpersonal and intrapersonal development" (Bertrand Jones et al., 2016, p. 12). It is important to keep in mind that in the dynamic process of learning leadership, identity and capacity inform one another (Guthrie et al., 2013), which leads to efficacy.

Similar to reflection and leadership, identity is also a socially constructed concept. Identity is grounded in historical, cultural, and political norms (Jones & Abes, 2013), that encompass multiple dimensions of self. Some social identities include gender, race, ethnicity, social class, age, or ability. Students can also develop their leader identity (Guthrie et al.,

2013). The culturally relevant leadership learning model "creates space for students to understand their leader identity within and through the lenses of their multiple and complex layers of identity" (Bertrand Jones et al., 2016, p. 13). Understanding identity requires intentional self-reflection by students, and leadership educators must reflect on the ways in which leadership programs include and welcome students with diverse identities. Reflection is important for leader identity development, and many of the factors that promote leader identity—including relationships, mentoring, self-assessment, and new experiences (Bertrand Jones et al., 2016)—are present in the reflection in leadership learning framework. Reflection on experiences and the support of mentors for processing and making meaning of experiences encourage leader identity development.

Capacity can be defined as integration of knowledge, skills, and attitudes (Dugan, 2017). This integration can influence an individual's overall ability to engage successfully in the leadership process. Developing leadership capacity stems from three core beliefs of leadership educators:

> The skills of leadership can and should be learned; that the learning and development of leadership capacities are inextricably intertwined; and that leadership educators can purposefully foster learning environments that help students integrate knowledge, skills, and experiences in meaningful ways. (Owen, 2012, p. 22)

Another way of framing the development of leadership capacity is in terms of knowing, being, and doing: knowing is studying effective leadership practice; being is the study of a leader's inner qualities; and doing is practicing the skills necessary to engage in the leadership process (Rosch & Anthony, 2012). Some specific interactions and experiences also facilitate capacity building. The Multi-Institutional Study of Leadership identified high-impact leadership experiences that enhance capacity (Dugan, Kodama, Correia, & Associates, 2013); these practices—which include sociocultural conversations with peers, mentoring relationships, community service, and memberships in off-campus organizations—invite reflection, either directly as part of the interaction or as a means of processing experience.

Leadership efficacy is "a student's beliefs about his or her abilities to exercise their leadership knowledge and skills in a given situation" (Denzine, 1999, p. 3). Leadership efficacy is impacted by messages that communicate normative assumptions about leadership, and "these messages can have particularly adverse effects on students from traditionally marginalized populations" (Dugan et al., 2013, p. 20). Students develop efficacy through meaningful experience, role modeling, supports, and emotional cues (Bandura, 1997; Komives, Wagner, & Associates, 2009), as well as positional leadership roles and sociocultural conversations (Dugan et al., 2013). Reflection is essential for processing experiences and can be included in sociocultural conversations. Leadership self-efficacy not only predicts capacity, it is a "factor in whether or not students actually enact leadership behaviors" (Dugan et al., 2013, p. 20). Deeply understanding how the interplay of identity, capacity, and efficacy impacts leadership learning helps educators develop effective programs.

At the heart of culturally relevant leadership learning is the focus of a leader's identity, capacity, and efficacy. However, the strength of culturally relevant leadership learning is also taking into consideration organizational and campus culture through five critical domains. These domains include: (a) historical legacy of inclusion and exclusion, (b) compositional diversity, (c) psychological climate, (d) behavioral climate, and (e) organizational/structural aspects (Bertrand Jones et al., 2016). By intentionally considering leadership learning opportunities from a campus climate perspective, educators are able to better understand the cultural context in which students are engaging in leadership learning. As Guthrie and Thompson (2010) pointed out, environments created on college campuses directly impact student learning. The culturally relevant leadership learning model acknowledges how external forces influence institutional contexts for leadership engagement. The five domains of culturally relevant leadership learning empower leadership educators to consider the importance of students' experiences with the broader campus climate and how students engage in the leadership learning context of the campus. Linking cultural relevance to leadership learning requires reflection, not only by educators who are creating leadership learning opportunities, but also by students who are engaging in the learning. Developing identity, capacity, and efficacy requires reflection on knowledge, skills, attitudes, and behaviors; understanding the impact of campus and organizational culture also necessitates significant time and energy for critical reflection, particularly for educators and students who may not have previously considered the impact of campus climate on leadership learning. By understanding the campus climate in which students are learning leadership, leadership educators can create intentional spaces for reflection.

IMPORTANCE OF REFLECTION IN LEADERSHIP LEARNING

Reflection is a mainstay for leadership learning. As we have demonstrated, reflection is a key connection between the leadership learning framework (Guthrie & Jenkins, 2018), which outlines developing intentional leadership learning opportunities for students, and the culturally relevant leadership learning model (Bertrand Jones et al., 2016), which demonstrates the criticality of educators and students understanding the context for leadership learning. When we look broadly at leadership learning, reflection ties all of these aspects together. Not only is reflection an essential aspect of all elements of the leadership learning framework, but it is an essential element of culturally relevant leadership learning (Bertrand Jones et al., 2016) in order to assist students in developing identity, capacity, and efficacy. If students understand and utilize reflection, they may engage in reflection more consistently in the leadership learning process, which may enhance their learning.

We hope this chapter expanded your thinking regarding how students learn leadership, and how reflection is essential for leadership learning. It is vital that educators come from a learner-centered perspective when creating leadership development programs in order to make students and their learning the focus of education. When we deeply understand how students learn leadership, it allows us to create stronger learning environments. These environments can enrich students' leadership capacity and assist them in thinking critically and strategically about engaging in the leadership process, especially through reflection.

CHAPTER 4

REFLECTIVE STRATEGIES FOR PEDAGOGY AND LEARNING ASSESSMENT

Leadership learning can take place in curricular and cocurricular settings. In this chapter, we focus on course-based experiential leadership learning while also highlighting cocurricular applications. Reflection is an important pedagogy for leadership learning, and it also serves as an outcome, instructional strategy, and learning assessment strategy. In chapter 2, we described how reflection and leadership are socially constructed phenomena; as such, reflection in leadership learning creates space for individual perspectives. Reflection on experience may include thoughts, feelings, and beliefs that can make it challenging for educators to assess reflection artifacts. However, with appropriate framing and a focus on demonstrated learning, educators may use reflection to assess leadership learning outcomes. Ash and Clayton (2004) noted the importance of reflection structures that allow students to demonstrate learning rather than describe what they learned. In this chapter, we offer possibilities for reflection in curricular settings including developing learning goals, planning instructional strategies, framing reflection, and assessing reflection artifacts.

EXPERIENTIAL LEADERSHIP LEARNING

In Chapter 2, we described experiential learning broadly, and here we focus on experiential leadership learning. Experiential learning draws on theoretical approaches that conceptualize learning as an active process.

Thinking to Transform: Reflection in Leadership Learning
pp. 63–79
Copyright © 2019 by Information Age Publishing

Rather than approaching instruction as imbuing students with knowledge, students are engaged in the learning process. The definition of leadership from Guthrie and Jenkins (2018) hinges on "educational experiences, both cocurricular and curricular in nature, associated with the activity of leadership" that, through a process of reflective learning, result in "changes in knowledge, skills, behavior, attitudes, and values" (p. 57). In Chapter 3, we described the leadership learning framework (Guthrie & Jenkins, 2018) where foundational leadership knowledge is attained through development, training, observation, and engagement; these elements are supported by metacognition and the ability to "think about one's thoughts" related to leadership.

Leadership learning is enhanced by environments that promote experiential learning and reflection. Guthrie and Thompson (2010) described the value of student and academic affairs partnerships that "provide a seamless learning environment for students to gain high quality leadership experiences" (p. 54). Leadership learning may take place in a classroom or cocurricular setting. Strong partnerships between curricular and cocurricular settings "are opportunities for leadership knowledge acquisition, practice application of leadership skills and knowledge, and reflection on the experiences in light of the education" (Guthrie & Thompson (2010, p. 54). To make experiences meaningful and educative, instructors should integrate reflection into courses and cocurricular settings, prioritize reflection with students, provide clear expectations for reflection and assessment criteria, and share feedback on the content and process of reflection. In order to embody reflection, educators must create experiences and environments that support and value this pedagogy (Guthrie & Jenkins, 2018). In short, "reflection is essential to applying leadership learning to students' lives" (White & Guthrie, 2016, p. 70).

Using reflection as a strategy for instruction and an assessment tool is embedded in the reflection in leadership learning framework. Many of the grounding elements of the framework lend themselves well to being developed in a curricular setting. Students need knowledge of leadership theory in order to draw meaningful connections to their own experiences through reflection. Simultaneously, students should gain experience that allows them to engage with diverse others, practice leadership skills, test leadership knowledge, and explore their values. Instructors can also expose students to reflection methods and engage them in developing a reflective practice by prioritizing time for reflection and not assuming students know how to reflect. The support structures of the reflection in leadership learning framework emphasize the importance of educators prioritizing time and space for reflection in curricular and cocurricular settings. Instructors can also provide appropriate challenge and support (Sanford, 1967) as well as substantive feedback. To bridge the gap between the classroom and the community, and help students learn the art of leadership, students should be engaged in experiential learning (Hughes, Ginnet, & Curphy, 2012). Instructors should identify learning goals that are supported by experiences and reflection. In a leadership education program, students should have multiple experiences that focus on addressing complex social issues and include exposure to diverse perspectives.

REFLECTION AS PEDAGOGY AND LEARNING ASSESSMENT

Over time, there have been many influences on theoretical frameworks, curriculum, and assessment strategies in leadership education. Additionally, leadership learning and development may be different from other content in a classroom setting meaning leadership education may require a unique pedagogy to facilitate learning (Eich, 2008; Komives, Lucas, & McMahon, 2013). Marzano (2007) identified three distinct components of effective classroom pedagogy: "1. Use of effective instructional strategies; 2. Use of effective classroom management strategies; [and] 3. Effective classroom curriculum design" (p. 5). First, to maximize the potential for developing students' leadership capacity, leadership educators should intentionally construct a course or program using clearly defined learning goals. These inform how educators identify experiences and pedagogies to actualize the learning goals. Educators can then connect relevant student and leadership development theories with the experiences. After identifying goals and experiences, leadership educators should sequence learning activities strategically, apply effective strategies to deliver the material to a diverse student population, and establish a robust set of assessment activities to measure student learning and development (Harper, 2011). Finally, leadership educators should use information from assessments to understand the developmental readiness (Avolio & Hannah, 2008) of students in their courses and programs. This can help educators choose developmentally appropriate strategies for building leadership identity, capacity, and efficacy (Bertrand Jones, Guthrie, & Osteen, 2016). Although programs constructed without this framework may still be successful, we advocate for this approach as one that maximizes instructional efficiency.

CURRICULUM DESIGN: LEARNING GOALS

Learning goals are an essential structural element of learning experiences. They create a framework that enables educators to select appropriate instructional strategies and develop assessments. Without clearly stated learning goals, it can be difficult to determine if leadership programs are effective and students are learning from experiences. Suskie (2018) specified learning goals "describe what students will be able to do as a result of a learning experience" whereas "learning outcomes are the knowledge, skills, attitudes, and habits of mind that students take with them from an experience" (p. 41). For leadership programs, learning goals may be influenced by a guiding framework or theory; national organization standards; university, divisional, or departmental mission; curriculum committee; strategic plan; or external sources. Learning based solely on experience, without reflection, may reinforce stereotypes, become frustrating if students do not glean the most important information from experiences, fail to develop students' capacity for acting on their learning, and provide only a partial understanding of the significance of those experiences (Ash & Clayton, 2004, 2009; Hatcher & Bringle, 1997). Reflection may be an instructional strategy that leads to outcomes, a means to assess outcomes, or an outcome in and of itself (Ward & McCotter, 2004).

In a grounded theory study of high-quality leadership programs, Eich (2008) found reflection activities were a key student-centered experiential learning opportunity. There were two learning outcomes associated with reflection activities that related to individual development and lifelong learning: "students learn more about themselves, develop future visions and goals, and become more purposeful with being themselves and making congruent decisions" and "students develop a meaningful leadership philosophy, model, or framework to analyze their own thoughts and actions to ultimately integrate improvements in their life and leadership" (Eich, 2008, p. 183). Building on the work of Eich (2008), Guthrie and Jenkins (2018) found one of the distinctive characteristics of high-quality leadership programs was intentional design which includes purposeful outcomes connected to appropriate instructional strategies. When designing learning outcomes, Ash and Clayton (2009) noted the importance of "beginning with the end in mind" (p. 29). To develop leadership capacity, leadership educators "must be intentional in matching their intended program or course outcomes with relevant student and leadership development theory, and then apply effective strategies for the delivery of material to a diverse student population" (Rosch & Anthony, 2012, p. 38). They suggested instructors identify learning goals and develop an overall strategy that may include multiple mechanisms or activities that are assessed (Ash & Clayton, 2009).

Learning taxonomies are a tool for developing learning goals. Although many people may be familiar with Bloom's (1956) taxonomy, which was revised by Anderson and Krathwohl (2001), there are several taxonomies that support developing outcomes. Suskie (2018) highlighted other taxonomies: dimensions of learning (Marzano, Pickering, & McTighe, 1993), the taxonomy of significant learning (Fink, 2013), and the taxonomy of educational objectives (Marzano & Kendall, 2008). When determining outcomes, educators should consider program duration, intended audience, and program sequence. For example, the outcomes for a 1-hour workshop may involve acquiring knowledge or remembering information whereas a capstone leadership course might have outcomes related to evaluating information or critical thinking. Reflection can be integrated into programs as a learning outcome such as "students will describe the role of reflection in leadership learning" or "students will practice multiple reflection methods." In other cases, reflection may be the instructional strategy that facilitates the development of leadership learning outcomes.

REFLECTIVE INSTRUCTIONAL STRATEGIES
FOR LEADERSHIP LEARNING

When planning for reflection, there are numerous activities that programs could incorporate; having options for activities is not a problem. Eyler (2001) pointed out "creating or borrowing reflection activities for service-learning classes is not difficult to do, but taking time to plan systematically for reflection appears to be rare" (p. 36); we maintain this is likely similar for other types of experiential learning, including leadership. Guthrie and Jenkins (2018) suggested leadership programs may be planned around the availability of certain facilitators or a schedule of activities that may not be related to specific outcomes. To respond to the challenge of too many activities without sufficient structure, Eyler (2001) proposed a reflection map as "a tool to help practitioners organize their thinking about integrating continuous reflective processes" (p. 36). A reflection map is a matrix organized by context (reflection alone, with classmates, or with community partners) and chronology (before service, during service, after service). Ash and Clayton (2009) described this process as a series of choices to produce an overall strategy that includes multiple reflection activities. Their questions about strategies include: "When and how often will reflection occur? Where will reflection occur? Who will facilitate and/or participate in reflect? How will feedback be provided and/or reflection products graded?" (Ash & Clayton, 2009, p. 34). Their questions for determining reflection mechanisms ask about learning goals, medium for the activity, prompts, products, and assessment criteria. This series of questions can be useful for planning and considering the overall reflection strategy for a course or program.

The processes from Eyler (2001) and Ash and Clayton (2009) describe service-learning could be easily adapted for leadership learning. For example, in a class where students work in small groups, reflection may take place individually, in groups to achieve a common goal, or as a whole class. Reflection could take place before groups are formed, during the group process, and after the project is completed. Other factors may influence the selection of instructional strategies including class size and whether the course is introductory or advanced. In planning for reflection throughout a course or program, educators may make use of multiple methods of reflection. For each element of the leadership learning framework, Guthrie and Jenkins (2018) provided suggestions for instruction and assessment. Some of the activities they identified, which may be used for reflective instruction or assessed to determine reflectivity, include:

- artwork,
- blogs,
- dialogue,
- discussion (face-to-face or online),
- internship,
- journaling,
- mind mapping,
- 1-minute paper,
- pair-share-report,
- presentation,
- role-play,
- service-learning,
- simulations,
- teambuilding or challenge course,
- theater,
- video reflection,
- vision board, and
- writing.

The selection of reflective instructional strategies should be influenced by the context for leadership program, the learning goals, and how instructional strategies contribute to the learning goals.

REFLECTION METHODS

For the purpose of this book and the companion manual, we grouped reflection methods into six categories: contemplative, creative, digital, discussion, narrative, and written. The methods should be considered in context. The utility of methods may vary based on curricular or cocurricular application. Here, we provide a brief overview of each category. In the companion manual to this book, a diverse group of scholar practitioners provided a rich collection of activities for reflection in leadership learning.

Contemplative

Often used synonymously with introspection or reflection, contemplative practices have an introspective or internal focus that facilitates insight (Barbezat & Bush, 2014). Practices such as meditation, mindfulness, walking the labyrinth, journaling, yoga, or deep listening can be used on their own or in combination with other strategies to facilitate understanding of self or connection to other materials (Barbezat & Bush, 2014). In examining college student spirituality, Astin, Astin, and Lindholm (2011) found "meditation and self-reflection enhance leadership development, and self-reflection is associated with enhanced intellectual self-esteem, strengthened commitment to promoting racial understanding, and greater self-rated ability to get along with other races and cultures" (p. 148). Lucas (2015) emphasized the importance of engaging students holistically to develop as leaders. She argued for mindfulness as a tool for increasing self-awareness and empathy in order to help students develop relational skills in addition to cognitive skills (Lucas, 2015).

Creative

Guthrie and Jenkins (2018) described the significance of art for leadership learning. Through both creating and interpreting art—including drawing, music, theater, visual art, and film, among others—students engage in holistic leadership learning that supports creativity and innovation. Parks Daloz, Keen, Keen, and Daloz Parks (1996) described the important role of artists for communities: in juxtaposing ideas, artists reveal truth and call attention to relationships. Both artisans and leaders reproduce the world, not only as they see it, but as they imagine it could be (Guthrie & Jenkins, 2018). In one example, McPherson and Mazza (2014) used arts-based activism in an undergraduate social work course focused on human rights. In another example, Huffaker and West (2005) used improv in a business classroom to engage students in risk taking and help them learn about creativity and leadership. When reflection results in a product, such as a composition, theater production, choreographed dance, or piece of art, those artifacts or presentations may be shared with stakeholders including other students, faculty, staff, administrators, or community partners.

Digital

In leadership, technology encompasses a range of digital spaces and tools that may influence leadership learning (Ahlquist & Endersby, 2017). Stoller (2013) argued social media spaces were as much "in real life" spaces as brick and mortar campuses, and administrators have an opportunity to join conversations and enhance connection through social media. As students and professionals navigate identity development, this includes negotiation of their digital identity or how they present themselves in online environments (Ahlquist, 2016; Gordon Brown, 2016). Blogs have been used for reflection in curricular and cocurricular settings including experiential learning (Ferguson, Makarem, & Jones, 2016), leadership classes (Gifford, 2010), study abroad (Savicki & Price, 2017), internships (Chu, Chan, & Tiwari, 2012), and community engagement (Hunt & Krakow, 2015). Guthrie and Meriwether (2018) applied a model for active learning in digital spaces to leadership development to frame guidelines for mentoring, coaching, and advising students. Through consistency, content management, and capturing measurable outcomes, educators can support collaborative, relational leadership learning in a digital sphere.

Discussion

Guthrie and Jenkins (2018) identified discussion as the signature pedagogy for leadership education. Both the content of the conversation and process of engaging with others are powerful elements of reflective discussion. Turkle (2015) described the importance of conversation for reflection:

> Face-to-face conversation is the most human—and humanizing—thing we do. Fully present to one another, we learn to listen. It's where we develop the capacity for empathy. It's where we experience the joy of being heard, of being understood. And conversation advances self-reflection, the conversations with ourselves that are the cornerstone of early development and continue throughout life. (p. 3)

Komives, Owen, Longerbeam, Mainella, and Osteen (2005) found reflective learning influenced students as they developed their leadership identity; one of the primary mechanisms for reflective learning was discussion, which began with meaningful conversation: "initially with a parent or sibling; participants described dinner table conversations, family meetings, and the listening ear of close-age siblings" (p. 598). Discussion is an important form of reflection. Through discussion leadership educators can challenge students and students can practice being in community as leaders and followers.

Narrative

A narrative is *"the representation of an event or a series of events"* (Abbott, 2008, p. 13, emphasis in original). The key feature of a narrative is the focus on an event (Abbott, 2008) which makes narratives well suited for reflecting on experiential learning. Moon (2010) referred to stories as "a unit of communication" that can take the form of "narrative, case study, critical incident, life history, anecdote, scenario, illustration or example, creative writing, [or] storytelling" (p. i). She went on to highlight the educational possibilities for stories as tools for communication, facilitating learning from experience, research, constructing knowledge, and transmitting culture, among others (Moon, 2010). One example of narrative reflection is testimonio. Testimonio is a unique form of storytelling because of its intentional inclusion of affirmation and empowerment (Latina Feminist Group, 2001; Reyes & Curry Rodríguez, 2012). Another form of narrative, poetry has significant power as a tool to prompt reflection because it utilizes evocative language to engage participants (Mazza, 2003). Poetry can support reflection in leadership learning by opening up dialogue about topics that can be uncomfortable for students to discuss and inviting creative responses to experiences.

Written

Writing is a powerful strategy for teaching because the writing process develops the writer and draws attention inward enabling self-awareness and making meaning of experience (Fink, 2013). Journaling is one of the most common reflection activities (Eyler, 2001). In some cases, journaling can provide an opportunity to explore emotions and emotional reactions (Moon, 2006). Journals are a place to sort out informational and transformational ideas; they prepare people for conversations with others and allow them to converse with themselves (Stevens & Cooper, 2009). In this way, journals are a solid complement to discussion because students can draw upon what they wrote instead of bringing only selected memories to the discussion (Astin, Vogelgesang, Ikeda, & Yee, 2000). A popular written reflection is the 1-minute paper (Angelo & Cross, 1993) which elicits a brief reflection at the end of an experience or class and provides formative assessment for educators. Digital and paper portfolios also enable learners to aggregate materials for reflection including both the products of reflection and the process of learning (Fernsten & Fernsten, 2005).

FRAMING REFLECTION AND MANAGING EXPECTATIONS

After crafting learning goals and determining instructional strategies, educators need to consider how they will implement reflection in the classroom. How educators frame reflection is significant. Engaging students in reflection requires structure and support from an experienced facilitator—telling students "it is now time to reflect" may not be sufficient (Welch, 1999, p.1). Owen-Smith (2018) described the potentially detrimental impact of expecting students to reflect on deep ideas without sufficient time or preparation. Without understanding or clarity, "one result of this fragmented use of reflection is an increase in student anxiety, sense of failure, and confusion around meaning-making and analyses" (Owen-Smith, 2018, p. 41). By providing structure and clarifying expectations, educators can support reflection and learning.

In studies where educators reviewed students' reflective work, one of the findings was a low level of reflective capacity (Hatton & Smith, 1995; Kember, McKay, Sinclair, & Wong, 2008; Ward & McCotter, 2004). In one example, when assessing essays from teacher education students, Hatton and Smith (1995) identified four types of reflection: descriptive writing, descriptive reflection, dialogic reflection, and critical reflection. Using a set of criteria to evaluate the essays, they found 60–70% of the reflection was descriptive and few students engaged in critical reflection (Hatton & Smith, 1995). In another example, Ward and McCotter (2004) developed a rubric that had four levels of reflection: routine, technical, dialogic, and transformative. Although few students attained the level of transformative reflection, Ward and McCotter (2004) suggested educators could use the rubric as a scaffold to facilitate students' movement to higher levels of abstract thinking.

Techniques to support reflection may be useful, particularly when students are resistant to reflection. One of the recommendations Beauchamp (2015) found in the literature was giving learners more control in order to facilitate deeper reflection. This echoes the learner-centered focus of leadership education (Guthrie & Jenkins, 2018). Learner control may allow students to engage in more meaningful reflection, and it may decrease hostility related to required reflection or performativity (Beauchamp, 2015). White (2012) found students who were required to write reflections with a minimum length sometimes felt compelled to elaborate on their experiences or exaggerate emotions, either to fulfill assignment criteria or based on assumed instructor expectations. Newcomb, Burton, and Edwards (2018) also found this to be true when engaging students with a history of childhood adversity in critical reflection. Students lacked authenticity in their reflection because of fear of judgment, the risks of disclosing emotions, and the constraints of academic assignments (Newcomb, Burton, & Edwards, 2018).

It is not enough to say "reflect" and expect students will be able to understand what is being asked of them. White (2014) found while some students were exposed to reflection prior to college, other students learned how to reflect through curricular and cocurricular experiences in college. Although on their own students may recall experiences, they may not progress to more advanced analysis, evaluation, or synthesis in their reflection without support. In addition to developing quality outcomes and planning instructional strategies appropriate for outcomes, educators need to manage the environment to facilitate reflective leadership learning. Some ways instructors can support student learning include framing reflection through prompts or scaffolding and managing expectations using rubrics.

Prompting or Scaffolding Reflection

Students are often asked to reflect without sufficient explanation; prompting reflection or providing clear guidelines may enhance reflection. A prompt is the "statement or question that tells students what they are to do" (Suskie, 2018, p. 211). Prompts are often a series of questions that direct the focus of reflection. Suskie (2018) provided a list of prompts for reflection on a learning experience, and here we highlight a few examples:

> What makes a person a good [leader]? What might you say if you have a chance to speak to your friends and family about this experience? What did you learn about [leadership] from this experience? What did you learn from this experience that is *not* reflected in your work? (p. 262, emphasis in original)

Although reflection can allow for creativity and exploration, prompts may help students frame reflections (Correia & Bleicher, 2008). Reflective prompts should "be phrased to elicit honest answers, with no obviously right or wrong answer" (Suskie, 2018, p. 264). For example, if students write in a journal weekly, educators might provide prompts or guiding questions each week. If an experience takes place over a semester, the prompts might require increasing cognitive and affective complexity as the semester progresses.

Another tool for framing reflection is scaffolding. Suskie (2018) defined scaffolding as "breaking an assignment into pieces or steps that are progressively challenging and giving students support as they work on each step of the process" (p. 211). Scaffolding is used "to help a learner undertake a task or goal that is beyond the present level of the learner's capacity" (Bean & Stevens, 2002, p. 208). Bean and Stevens (2002) described multiple features of scaffolding for cognitive and affective learning that focused on choosing appropriate challenges, observing efforts and providing support where needed, creating an atmosphere that allowed for mistakes, and engaging with students to provide hints or feedback. As socially constructed processes, both reflection and leadership may be challenging for students to define; as we saw in our survey, the definitions of both represented a wide range of philosophical approaches to the topics. Having a shared understanding of expectations for reflection and a supportive environment may help students write about new or unfamiliar concepts.

Using Rubrics for Reflection

Rubrics can be useful for evaluating reflective work; they can also be useful for framing expectations for reflection. To begin, "a *rubric* is a written guide for assessing student work" (Suskie, 2018, p. 190). Suskie (2018) outlined varying rubrics in education. From the most basic to the more advanced, rubrics build upon one another: checklists (a list of things that should be present), rating scales (a checklist with the addition of a scale to judge frequency or quality), and analytic rubrics (a rating scale that includes brief descriptions rather than check boxes). Analytic rubrics "might be the gold standard because they document standards for student performance explicitly" (Suskie, 2018). An analytic rubric may provide levels of reflection with a description for each. For example, Ward and McCotter (2004) created a rubric with four columns (routine, technical, dialogic, and transformative) and three rows (focus, inquiry, and change). In each cell, at the intersection of a row and a column, they included a brief description of what would characterize that type of reflection.

Though matrices or rubrics are often used to evaluate student work, Hubbs and Brand (2010) suggested a matrix could serve as both an evaluative instrument as well as a tool to provide instructors and students with a common language for reflection. By showing students visually the continuum of reflection on the matrix (one axis focused on content and process; the other axis ranging from superficial to deep analysis) they could frame expectations for journal entries. Similarly, in looking for specific types of connections in student reflections, Correia and Bleicher (2008) found the use of "reflection markers" or specific words or phrases (for example "I never thought …") useful in identifying the different types of connections. These reflection markers became tools for discussions with students in order to further learning and reflection (Correia & Bleicher, 2008).

Between 2007 and 2009, the Association of American College and Universities developed a series of rubrics as part of the Liberal Education and America's Promise initiative. The Valid Assessment of Learning in Undergraduate Education (VALUE) rubrics are a tool for assessment that can be used across disciplines (Rhodes, 2010). Although there is a not a rubric for leadership, there are a number of rubrics related to content important for leadership learning including teamwork, critical thinking, civic engagement, and foundations and skills for lifelong learning (Rhodes, 2010). These rubrics, or a modified version of these, could be used to evaluate student learning and development.

ASSESSING AND EVALUATING REFLECTION IN LEADERSHIP LEARNING

Leadership is both socially constructed and personal which can make it challenging for educators to assess leadership learning. At the same time, Dugan (2012) implored "the work of leadership development is only as strong as educators' abilities to document student learning" (p. 99). Guthrie and Jenkins (2018) provided instructional strategies and guidelines for assessment for each element of the leadership learning framework. They noted "effective leadership educators choose assessments that are reflective of their learning outcomes, responsive to the needs of their students, and authentic to their own values as well" (Guthrie & Jenkins, 2018, p. 63). Preston and Peck (2016) challenged leadership educators to align assessments with values in order to "produce student-centered assessment" (p. 79). They cautioned that the assessment method should depend upon the experience, not the other way around. Finally, they argued for a focus on qualitative assessments which are useful for understanding the lived experiences of students; qualitative assessments can also be reflective by their nature (Preston & Peck, 2016). Regardless of the outcomes or methods selected, Guthrie and Jenkins (2018) recommended, "employing assessments appropriate for the leadership learning context and combining strategies in innovative and creative ways to better determine what and how students learn leadership" (p. 63).

Reflection as assessment can benefit students and educators: educators can assess student learning, which can be used to improve teaching and learning, and students can use reflection on experiences to self-assess learning (Hatcher & Bringle, 1997). Ash and Clayton (2009) noted reflection provides an opportunity for formative assessment (used along the way to improve the reflection process) and summative assessment (used to evaluate processes and document outcomes). In order to assess experiential learning, educators need to develop reflection that addresses desired learning outcomes and incorporate assessment into the process of reflection (Ash & Clayton, 2009). Assessing reflection entails a series of decisions on the part of educators: what will be assessed, how frequently, and with what standards. One challenge for reflection as a learning assessment is students may be uncomfortable sharing honestly, particularly if their reflection artifacts are being assessed for a grade. Eyler and Giles (1999) described instances where privately experiential learners gave critical or negative feedback, but publicly they shared positive reflections on an experience. In some cases, students may be afraid to share honestly because they do not want to be viewed negatively by the instructor. By attending to the power dynamic that exists in a classroom setting, instructors can create a safe space for honest reflections and diffuse the tension inherent in submitting reflective materials for a grade. Eyler and Giles (1999) asserted "if we want to make full educational use of the advantages of immersing students in complex and messy real-world situations, we cannot create classrooms where it is unacceptable to share shock, disappointment, or confusion" (p. 202). In Chapter 6, we discuss the power dynamic between students and educators that may influence reflection. Here, we discuss grading reflective work and providing feedback on reflection.

Grading Reflective Work

As noted above, the classroom environment is significant and may influence the degree to which students feel comfortable sharing reflections, particularly when these reflections are being graded. Fernsten and Fernsten (2005) noted reflections may negatively impact students whose ideas are incongruent with instructor expectations. They cautioned instructors that "to chastise or discipline students for including information that one does not like hearing in a reflection is counterproductive to the reflective process" (Fernsten & Fernsten, 2005, p. 304). Walmsley and Birkbeck (2006) found many students who completed reflective journals as part of an international social work course "were unhappy with the evaluative aspect of the assignment. Both focus groups talked about the potential to feel judged and fears about the sensitive nature of the information and the power such knowledge could give the instructor" (p. 122). In some cases, students may feel pressured to figure out what instructors prefer and sacrifice honest reflections for a potentially higher grade (O'Connell & Dyment, 2011). Templates or rubrics may facilitate fairer grading of students' reflective materials (Garrity, 2013). Hubbs and Brand (2010) suggested assessment of reflective writing should be on the reflection process and student learning, not the content and student performance.

Stevens and Cooper (2009) offered suggestions for educators addressing the dilemma of grading reflective journals; these suggestions could apply to other reflection artifacts. To counter concerns and encourage deep, critical reflection, Stevens and Cooper (2009) contended educators need to create environments where students feel safe expressing beliefs or assumptions. One of their suggestions for creating a safe environment was to check journals for completion without reading the content. However, checking for completion compromises an opportunity to be actively engaged with students, guide learning, and provide feedback. Another option is to provide a rubric or criteria for grading journals (Stevens & Cooper, 2009). As mentioned above, a benefit to providing students with criteria for grading reflections is it opens a conversation and ensures educators and students are speaking a similar language as it relates to reflection and expectations for reflection artifacts (Hubbs & Brand, 2010).

Suskie (2018) concurred, "Grading student reflections may stifle that honesty, encouraging students to write only what they think we want to hear instead of what they truly think and feel" (p. 264). However, grades may also incentivize students to write careful reflections. Some grading for underlying elements could focus on "evidence of thinking skills such as analysis and synthesis; effort in completing the assignment thoughtfully; meaningfulness of personal responses and opinions; or connecting one's opinions to what has been learned in the course, program or cocurricular experience" (Suskie, 2018, p. 265). There are a number of factors to consider in whether or not to grade reflection artifacts including the power dynamic in the classroom, the potentially personal nature of reflection in leadership learning, and how the knowledge that their work is being graded may impact students. Educators should consider these factors in the context of the program and the learning outcomes to determine if they should grade reflection artifacts and how they should approach the process.

Providing Feedback

Feedback is an integral component of leadership learning, and it plays a pivotal role in helping students make meaning of experience (Guthrie & Jenkins, 2018). Feedback is salient for reflection in curricular and cocurricular leadership learning. In the broadest sense, "feedback includes any information you get about yourself" (Stone & Heen, 2014, p. 4). Educational feedback is "information provided by an agent (e.g., teacher, peer, book, parent, self, experience) regarding aspects of one's performance or understanding" (Hattie & Timperley, 2007, p. 81); this is typically shared following instruction to support the development of knowledge, skills, and values (Hattie & Timperley, 2007). Conger (1992) highlighted the importance of feedback as a transformational instructional strategy. Particularly when incorporated regularly and early in the process, "through effective feedback processes, we can learn about our strengths and weaknesses in a number of leadership skills" (p. 50). Feedback can come from educators, and it can also come from peers (Guthrie & Jenkins, 2018). Stone and Heen (2014) noted feedback is "how we learn about ourselves from our experiences and from other people—how we learn about life" (p. 4); in this vein, feedback is closely related to reflection in leadership learning.

Fink (2013) highlighted feedback and assessment as integral components of integrated course design. She advocated for "educative assessment" which goes beyond traditional assessments that audit learning and noted, "most teachers do not know how to go beyond grading to be able to provide the kinds of feedback and assessment that will enhance the learning process itself" (Fink, 2013, p. 93). Fink (2013) distinguished feedback from assessment by the fact that feedback is not part of the course grade and feedback happens through dialogue with learners. She developed an acronym for education feedback: FIDeLity feedback is feedback that is "*f*requent, *i*mmediate, *d*iscriminating [based on clear criteria and standards], and delivered *l*ovingly" (Fink, 2013, p. 94). The process of giving and receiving feedback has the potential to be reflective. For the person giving feedback, it requires seeing someone or their work and considering observations in the context of criteria which may be either expressly stated or internalized. Next the person must formulate what they will share, and educators often strive to balance praise or affirmation with constructive feedback. Although it may be more challenging to provide feedback that corrects misperceptions or challenges entrenched ideas, this is significant educative feedback. After sharing the feedback, verbally or in writing, the educator can observe for follow up. When people are on the receiving end of feedback, they can incorporate this with their own thoughts as they revisit what happened and try to understand the meaning of the experience. Learners can apply feedback to future actions through new or modified actions or beliefs before evaluating the impact of these changes. In this way, the process of feedback mirrors the process of reflection.

FROM BLUEPRINT TO STRUCTURE:
DESIGNING REFLECTIVE LEADERSHIP LEARNING

Although a skilled facilitator or an experienced educator may be able to make effective leadership learning seem easy, developing leadership learning experiences requires time and energy. Experiential educators embrace the idea that learners are not vessels to be filled but individuals whose lifelong learning ability can be cultivated. Rather than giving students a blank slate for reflection, educators should create a framework that supports reflection by managing expectations, providing prompts, scaffolding instructions, and providing feedback. This process is similar to building a structure. First, you need a blueprint that outlines the plan and sets the direction. This is similar to developing a strategy for reflection. After laying a solid foundation, the support structures and walls are built. In our metaphor, this represents the guidance provided by educators in the form of scaffolding, prompts, and feedback. As we provide framing and structure for learners, we also hope to empower them with the knowledge and skills required to make reflection a lifelong practice. Using reflection as a pedagogical tool requires managing the ambiguity that comes with not having a correct answer but opens up the possibility of unforeseen and profoundly meaningful exchanges that facilitate learning. Leadership learning is enhanced by reflection which is planned thoughtfully and incorporated skillfully. Reflection is integral to leadership learning as a pedagogy, instructional strategy, learning goal, and assessment tool.

CHAPTER 5

CRITICAL REFLECTION IN LEADERSHIP LEARNING

Leadership is both interdisciplinary and multidisciplinary; reflection is important philosophically and practically for making meaning of experiences and learning about leadership. The constructivist approach to both reflection and leadership creates opportunities for lived experiences to be included because of the value placed on individual meaning making. The culturally relevant leadership learning model (Bertrand Jones, Guthrie, & Osteen, 2016) focuses on including all students in the leadership process. Similarly, reflection should be approachable for and inclusive of all learners so they can process cognitive and affective responses to leadership experiences for learning and understanding broader social structures. At the same time, reflection should be challenging to encourage learners to recognize and question assumptions.

We advocate for a reciprocal and symbiotic relationship between reflection and leadership: leadership requires reflection to understand systems; reflection on leadership learning that results in taking action for social change reclaims the role of reflection as a means to societal transformation. In this chapter, we explore the distinction between reflection and critical reflection. We also look at how critical reflection enables a deep and connected understanding that enables leaders to create positive change with communities. Reflection and action are connected; the core tenants of leadership as experiential and active, and the consideration for identity and community, open up possibilities for justice-oriented action that is the pinnacle of reflective praxis. We believe

Thinking to Transform: Reflection in Leadership Learning
pp. 81–98
Copyright © 2019 by Information Age Publishing
All rights of reproduction in any form reserved.

dynamic leadership learning experiences and support for critical reflection can lead to the development of identity, capacity, and efficacy; knowledge about the role of political and social structures in learning; transformation of assumptions and beliefs; and a shift in perspective that incites action for change. In this chapter, we explore critical reflection, propose a continuum of critical reflection, and describe elements of learning that contribute to critical reflection.

NOT ALL REFLECTION IS CRITICAL

Critical reflection is often used to describe deeper or more complex thinking; however, similar to reflection, this term is often vaguely defined or misapplied (Beauchamp, 2015). In developing an operational framework, which looked for evidence of different types of reflection in written work, Hatton and Smith (1995) noted "critical reflection, like reflection itself, appears to be used loosely, some taking it to mean no more than constructive self-criticism of one's actions with a view to improvement" (p. 35). In this chapter, we describe a continuum of critical reflection; before we do this, it is useful to clarify what critical reflection is *not*. Experiential learning literature includes many instances where the terms reflection and critical reflection are comingled; here we provide a few examples.

When citing Dewey's (1933) seminal definition of reflection, some scholars suggest Dewey was referring to *critical* reflection while others cite his definition as one for reflection. In another example, Jacoby (2015) defined critical reflection in service-learning as "the process of analyzing, reconsidering, and questioning one's experiences within a broad context of issues and content knowledge" (p. 26). She went on to say the term "critical" was useful to as a reminder that reflection was *critical* to service-learning, reflection must be well executed to develop *critical* thinking skills, reflection could raise *critical* questions, and *critical reflection* was the foundation of *critical* service-learning (Jacoby, 2015). Although all of these applications are true and important, the overuse of the word critical may be seen as watering down critical reflection. This is similar to the confusion that results from "carelessly interchanging the language of the person (leaders) and the process (leadership)" (Guthrie & Jenkins, 2018, p. 5). Educators must continue to explore the tension between belaboring conversations about definitions and upholding conceptual clarity that supports scholarship and practice.

In leadership literature, Densten and Gray (2001) incorporated elements of criticality in their definition of critical reflection; however, people who cite their definition often drift from the clarity and complexity of the original definition. In looking at these examples and others, we support Brookfield's (2009) assertion; "conflating of the terms 'reflection' and 'critical reflection' implies that adding the qualifier 'critical' somehow makes the kind of reflection happening deeper and more profound" (p. 294). The terms "reflection" and "critical reflection" should not be used interchangeably. Although all critical reflection is reflection, not all reflection is critical. Distinguishing between approaches to reflection is useful for setting expectations. Additionally, facilitating increasingly complex critical reflection may require more intentional self-work on the part of educators in order to help learners understand experiences in context and develop knowledge, skills, and values through considering their beliefs (Guthrie & Jenkins, 2018). By using the terms reflection and critical reflection interchangeably, rather than elevating all reflection, it increases confusion and misrepresents critical reflection.

CRITICAL REFLECTION

Critical reflection has been used to describe a range of thought processes from technical reflection to reflection that invokes critical thinking or draws on critical social theory. In this chapter, we outline a continuum of critical reflection that places these concepts relative to one another and demonstrates the cognitive complexity required for critical reflection. Thompson and Pascal (2012) pointed out the significance of developing "a critical approach that addresses the depth and breadth aspects of criticality and the interrelationships between the two" (p. 322). They highlighted gaps where theorists including Schön (1983), whose work on reflection-in-action is used broadly, did not address social and political context, the role of emotions, or the role of power (Thompson & Pascal, 2012). Brookfield (2000) was clear: "For me the word *critical* is sacred and I object to its being thrown around indiscriminately" (p. 126, emphasis in original). He elaborated, "For something to count as an example of critical learning, critical analysis, or critical reflection, I believe that the persons concerned must engage in some sort of power analysis of the situation or context in which the learning is happening" (Brookfield, 2000, p. 126). Kilminster, Zukas, Bradbury, and Frost (2010) called attention to the role of power in reflection: as reflection has shifted from the margins to become a central practice in professions, there are concerns regarding "social tensions between professional autonomy and professional accountability; pressures for personal accountability and control; managerialism and audit cultures; and different understandings of learning" (p. 2). In a broader sense, a power analysis, which is essential to critical approaches to theory, would consider both the content and process of reflection as well as the influence of multiple actors in framing reflection.

Critical reflection shifts learners beyond their own experience to analysis that is grounded in context and acknowledges the significant impact of social and political context. Leadership learning invites learners to question assumptions about identity and social factors. Leadership and critical reflection provide mutually reinforcing structures that can elevate reflective thought to critical reflection which is actionable at the individual, institutional, and social levels.

CONTINUUM OF CRITICAL REFLECTION

Critical reflection is often applied in place of reflection without a description for what makes reflection critical. "Critical" is not a modifier that elevates all reflection. Considering context, content, process, and outcomes, we explore manifestations of critical reflection and their application to leadership learning on a continuum (Figure 5.1). The work of some authors spans multiple points on the continuum; our goal is not to categorize work, but to show representations of the many ways critical reflection is discussed in the literature. Our hope is to encourage educators to consider how they are incorporating critical elements into reflection and to use accurate terminology to represent learning goals. We also hope this continuum serves as a tool for educators who seek to intentionally engage learners in experiences and reflection that challenges them to practice leadership in ways that are complex and active.

On a continuum, the differences between adjacent elements are small, however the two ends of the continuum are quite distinct. The continuum

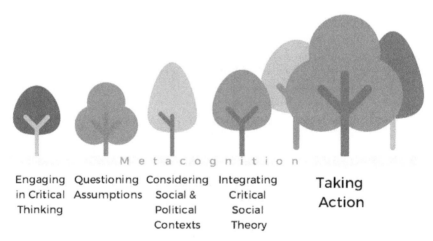

FIGURE 5.1. Continuum of critical reflection in leadership learning.

of critical reflection in leadership learning captures a range of possibilities for integrating complex contextual information as part of the reflection process. To begin, we discuss metacognition, which underscores the continuum. Metacognition is thinking about our thought process, or thinking about thinking (Kemmis, 1985). Moving from left to right along the continuum, each point involves increasing awareness of external structures that impact reflection on experiences in context. The first element on the continuum is engaging in critical thinking: in the most straightforward sense, critical reflection includes reflection that is informed by critical thinking. Next, we describe critical reflection that involves questioning assumptions and beliefs. After that is reflection that considers social and political contexts. The following element is reflection that incorporates critical social theory. Finally, at its most integrated, critical reflection can become a catalyst to take action for justice.

Metacognition

Fogarty and Pete (2018) described metacognition as "awareness and control over your own thinking" (p. viii). They gave an example: if you are reading some material and get to the end and realize you do not know what you just read so you go back and read the section again to get the content, "this awareness—knowing what you know and what you don't know—is called metacognition" (Fogarty & Pete, 2018, p. vii). Metacognition is rooted in psychology (Flavell, 1976) and the thinking skills movement of the 1980s (Fogarty & Pete, 2018). It includes self-knowledge and self-regulation or having an accurate sense of self, which are components of emotional intelligence (Goleman, 1998), paired with "the capacity to monitor and control our own cognitive processes" (Lau, 2015, p. 383). Metacognition emphasizes awareness of what one knows; this awareness supports the reflection process.

Fogarty and Pete (2018) described three aspects of metacognition: planning, monitoring and evaluating. Planning takes place in advance of an experience or event: "during this preparation time, it's almost as if you are standing *outside* the situation looking in" (Fogarty & Pete, 2018, p. viii, emphasis in original). Monitoring takes place in the moment in tandem with cognitive processes. For example, if an instructor is delivering content to students and notices blank stares or disengagement, they might shift strategies; "this monitoring of the students' reactions and the resulting adjustment to the instructional input is metacognitive in nature" (Fogarty & Pete, 2018, p. ix). Evaluating is where metacognition and reflection intersect. When we move beyond recalling something to considering how we learned the information: "This evaluative thinking—assessing what you know, and how you know it—is metacognitive thinking. Thinking about how you learn and being able to generalize those skills and strategies for transfer and use into diverse situations—that's metacognitive reflection" (Fogarty & Pete, 2018, p. ix). Guthrie and Jenkins (2018) centered metacognition in the leadership learning framework as an important element to support leadership development, training, observation, and engagement.

Ash and Clayton (2009) leaned on metacognitive processes to shift reflection beyond superficial "naval gazing" in order to become analytical and transformative: "critical reflection is an evidence-based examination of the sources of and gaps in knowledge and practice, with the intent to improve both" (Ash & Clayton, 2009, pp. 27–28). By becoming aware of both sources of knowledge and how knowledge is reproduced, metacognition can support reflection. In their framework for scaffolding reflection, Coulson and Harvey (2013) included metacognition as both a capacity to be developed as students learn to reflect and a skill to be applied as students reflect on action. Metacognition may also support incorporating critical social theory into leadership learning. Dugan (2017) highlighted the significance of this: "Metacognition is an essential skill ... because it allows us to explore not just *what* we know or *how* we know, but also the ways these are informed by stocks of knowledge, ideology/hegemony, and social location" (p. 49). Metacognition is an important learning strategy that can support critical reflection at all points along the continuum.

ENGAGING IN CRITICAL THINKING

Critical thinking is important for higher education; it is an element of career readiness, a key competency for students (National Association of Colleges and Employers, 2019), and a prevalent learning outcome. Although the term critical thinking is used broadly in education, it can be challenging to define. The National Association of Colleges and Employers (2019) described critical thinking/problem solving as the ability to "exercise sound reasoning to analyze issues, make decisions, and overcome problems. The individual can obtain, interpret, and use knowledge, facts, and data to solve problems, and may demonstrate originality and inventiveness." In the Association of American Colleges & Universities (2009) VALUE rubric, critical thinking is defined as "a habit of mind characterized by the comprehensive exploration of issues, ideas, artifacts, and events before accepting or formulating an opinion or conclusion" (Definition section, para. 1). Davies (2015) outlined cognitive elements of critical thinking (skills for argumentation and making judgments) and propensity elements of critical thinking (the disposition or frame of mind to exercise critical thinking). These ideas emerged from the critical thinking movement and focused more on the individual than the sociocultural dimensions (Davies, 2015) which we explore further along the continuum.

In his early work on transformative learning, Mezirow (1990) said "critical thinking is informed by critical reflection" and he equated critical thinking to reflective learning (p. xvii). On the other hand, some scholars said critical thinking was a prerequisite for deeper levels of reflection (Ash & Clayton, 2009; Ash, Clayton, & Atkinson, 2005). Ash and Clayton (2009) highlighted the importance of critical thinking for enhancing reflection and mitigating potentially problematic outcomes such as reinforcing stereotypes or failing to consider complexity. They argued to enhance student learning, reflection should be structured to facilitate increasingly complex thought while also improving the quality of thinking and reasoning (Ash & Clayton, 2009). In teaching students about controversy with civility as part of the social change model (Higher Education Research Institute, 1996), Alvarez (2017) encouraged leadership educators to include critical thinking questions to advance the conversation; however, they cautioned "the use of the concept of 'critical' means analyzing and interpreting assumptions, not making disapproving comments" (p. 159). Though potentially obvious for leadership educators, this may be an important distinction to make when educating students about critical thinking. Owen (2016) pointed out critical thinking focuses on applying logic and is politically neutral whereas critical reflection goes beyond critical thinking by considering the nature and sources of power, representation, voice, who benefits and who is silenced, distinctions between charity and change, and systemic oppression. Critical thinking and critical reflection are not interchangeable; however, elements of critical thinking support critical reflection.

Questioning Assumptions

One of the functions of critical reflection is engaging learners in questioning and recalibrating beliefs. This function is closely tied to transformative learning and prepares students to consider multiple perspectives as part of critical social theory. Mezirow (1990) viewed critical reflection as a trigger for transformative learning because it "involves a critique of the presuppositions on which our beliefs have been built" (p. 1). As an experiential pedagogy, service-learning has a significant focus on helping students question assumptions. Eyler and Giles (1999) pointed out the importance of critical reflection for engaged learners "to go beyond merely assimilating to the status quo" in order to "explore their assumptions that underlie their own perceptions and the way that society is organized" (p. 198). For example, students might initially reflect on serving at a shelter for persons experiencing homelessness but then go beyond their initial reactions to consider what underlying social issues might influence access to housing. In leadership learning, students might begin by reflecting on an experience, such as an event, and go beyond thinking about the success or failure to consider how members of the team interacted or how their work contributed to or inhibited the group process.

To facilitate questioning assumptions by social work students, Campbell and Baikie (2013) developed an approach called critically reflective analysis. This social justice focused approach was adapted from the Fook and Gardener (2007) model of critical reflection in combination with experience facilitating diversity trainings; the analysis focused on "fundamental values, assumptions, and beliefs" rather than behaviors (Campbell & Baikie, 2013, p. 453). In looking at leadership development through service-learning, Owen (2016) explored the role of perspective transformation. Drawing on Mezirow (1991) and Cranton (2002), she outlined the role of reflection in facilitating learners' exploration of assumptions and critical reflection on experiences. Experiential leadership learning, particularly engagement with the community, can challenge a student's worldview; with support from educators and reflection, students may be able to engage in deeper learning that results in perspective transformation.

According to Mezirow (1990), the most significant learning experiences in adulthood involve critical reflection. Transformative learning is the process "by which we transform our taken-for-granted frames of reference ... to make them more inclusive, discriminating, open, emotionally capable of change, and reflective so that they may generate beliefs and opinions that will prove more true or justified to guide action" (Mezirow, 2012, p. 76). Critical reflection is essential to transformative learning; through critical reflection, learners assess the validity of assumptions including the sources of beliefs and the consequences of acting on these (Mezirow, 1990). There are four ways by which learning occurs, all of which are supported by critical reflection: "by elaborating existing frames of reference, by learning new frames of reference, by transforming points of view, or by transforming habits of mind" (Mezirow, 2012, p. 84). Transformative learning requires reflection, however, not all reflection results in transformation (Brookfield, 2000).

In discussing the role of critical reflection in evaluating assumptions, or "the taken-for-granted beliefs about the world and our place within it that guide our actions," Brookfield (2017) described three types of assumptions: paradigmatic, prescriptive, and causal (p. 5). Paradigmatic assumptions are "the structuring assumptions we use to order the world into fundamental categories" and are the most difficult to recognize (p. 5). Prescriptive assumptions are grounded in paradigmatic assumptions and frame "what we *think* ought to be happening in a particular situation" (p. 6, emphasis in original). Causal assumptions, the easiest to uncover, are "assumptions about how different parts of the world work and about the conditions under which these can be changed" (p. 7). The consistent, regular examination of assumptions, "that's the discipline of critical reflection" (p. 7). Brookfield (2017) noted much of our daily reflection is technical; however, these "technical decisions become critical when we start to see them in their social or political context, influenced by the structures and workings of power that exist outside the classroom" (p. 9).

Considering Social and Political Contexts

Moving along the continuum of critical reflection in leadership learning, questioning assumptions and reconsidering beliefs may prompt learners to consider social and political contexts. Although critical thinking is politically neutral, reflection that addresses belief structures often intersects with beliefs about social and political issues which should be considered in context. Although reflection is rooted in social critiques, over time as the practice has become more mainstream in education and professions, it has shifted to a more individual pursuit (Kilminster et al., 2010). Kemmis (1985) called reflection "a political act, which either hastens or defers the realization of a more rational, just, and fulfilling society" (p. 140). In this conception, reflection goes beyond internal processes and connects to larger systems. Kemmis (1985) highlighted the political nature of reflection including how reflection, like language, is social and not purely individual; reflection shapes, and is shaped by, ideology. Reflection is an expression of power to construct society through communication and decision making, among others (Kemmis, 1985). In developing a framework for assessing reflective journals, Hatton and Smith (1995) identified four types of writing. The first reported facts, the second used personal judgments to provide reasons, and the third included discourse with self. Only the final level, critical, provided reasons for "decisions or events which takes account of the broader historical, social, and/or political contexts" (pp. 40–41). The criteria for recognizing writing with critical reflection included "demonstrates an awareness that actions and events are not only located in, and explicable by, reference to multiple perspectives but are located in, and influenced by multiple historical, and sociopolitical contexts" (Hatton & Smith, 1995, p. 49). Reflection that goes beyond the learner to consider a larger context may require additional support from educators to frame and support reflection.

In service-learning, some faculty have become aware of the problematic nature of reflection that is devoid of context. Reflection that does not consider power structures and may lead to the replication of assumptions (Mitchell, Donahue, & Young-Law 2012). At Florida State University, scholar practitioners who work with college students mentoring in local K–12 schools noticed a pattern of students expressing pity or blaming parents for "not caring about their children." They developed a reflection curriculum for service-learning students in a college of education course to introduce context into reflections on their service. Through a sequence of activities, students confront assumptions, approach communities using an asset-based lens, consider intersecting challenges (such as parents having multiple jobs, lack of transportation, students not having consistent access to food or other resources, etc.), and identify problematic narratives in their service experiences. Asset-based community development "should discover and mobilize skills, talents, and resources that exist right now in local people associations, and institutions" (Hamerlinck & Plaut, 2014, p. 2). Asset-based approaches are driven by relationships and rely on community strength before outside expertise (Hamerlinck & Plaut, 2014). In addition to providing an opportunity for preservice teachers to examine their assumptions and beliefs, these teachers can hopefully practice leadership in their field by infusing context-driven reflections on practice into education.

Some models and frameworks for leadership consider community contexts. The social change model (Higher Education Research Institute, 1996) includes a community/societal value of citizenship where "active community participation results from a sense of responsibility to the communities in which people live" (Bonnet, 2017, p. 176). Bonnet (2017) identified key elements of citizenship including social capital, awareness of community history, empowerment and privilege, social perspective taking, and coalition building. Understanding these elements requires reflection and self-examination of the ways in which people benefit from and perpetuate community systems. The culturally relevant leadership learning model (Bertrand Jones et al., 2016) emphasizes the role of five critical domains which impact leader identity, capacity, and efficacy. These domains—that include (a) historical legacy of inclusion and exclusion, (b) compositional diversity, (c) psychological climate, (d) behavioral climate, and (e) organizational/structural aspects—are heavily influenced by social and political context (Bertrand Jones et al., 2016). Leadership educators' ability to develop students may be enhanced by reflection on their campus climate in each of these domains. Dugan (2017) noted the importance of social perspective taking in leadership learning; in order to apply critical perspectives, learners should be able to consider other points of view which may support understanding and developing empathy.

Integrating Critical Social Theory

Although some conceptions of critical reflection invite learners to consider experiences in context, an approach to reflection that integrates critical social theory ensures consideration of power, privilege, and systems. As learners engage in critical reflection that examines information in the context of politics and critical theory, there is a greater impetus to move beyond thought to action that creates positive social change. Kreber (2012) distinguished "traditional critical thinking" that separates thought and action from the work of critical theorists who "seek not only to understand and solve complex problems but also to transform consciousness and practice" (p. 325). Kreber (2012) also noted, "It is this critical theory tradition that connects reflection explicitly with social and political purposes and ideology critique, and hence makes it *critical*" (p. 324, emphasis in original). Davies (2015) mapped the critical thinking movement, the criticality movement, and the critical pedagogy movement in order to demonstrate their overlap and distinctions; while critical thinking is largely concerned with individual work, such as individual skills or dispositions, critical pedagogy includes broader awareness of oppression and resistance to oppression that lead to critical participation.

Liu (2015) pointed out the importance of action to internalize perspective changes from critical reflection and transformative learning. Although reflection is often thought of as a cerebral activity, there is value in taking action as part of the process. To engage in justice learning, experiential leadership courses should incorporate critical reflection that "demands that experiences and issues be examined in light of social and political forces, link explicitly to further social action, and reveal hegemonic ideology—that is, the influence of unquestioned dominant cultures and philosophies" (Owen, 2016, p. 39). Mitchell (2008) described critical service-learning as "a critical approach that is unapologetic in its aim to dismantle structures of injustice" (p. 50), and arguably the same could be said of critical reflection that incorporates critical social theory. Critical reflection that incorporates critical social theory also shifts thinking from a singular activity to something the influences the collective. McNaughton (2016) described the goals of critical reflection informed by critical theory: "From a critical theory perspective, personal transformation or learning is not the principal end of critical reflection, but secondary to the primary goal of transforming society" (p. 297).

Leadership is also concerned with types of power and the role of power in relationships and actions. In his analysis, Brookfield (2017) examined the role of power structures in the classroom. Brookfield (2017) identified two purposes of critical reflection: illuminating power and uncovering hegemony. Illuminating power includes questioning the assumptions of dominant ideologies and exploring power dynamics in large-scale systems and institutions as well as individual interactions (Brookfield, 2017). Hegemony is "the process by which an existing order secures the consent of people to the legitimacy of the order, even when it disadvantages them greatly" (Brookfield, 2017, p. 39). These assumptions can be "elusive in their ordinariness" (Brookfield, 2017, p. 59). Mitchell et al. (2012) wrote about service-learning as a pedagogy of Whiteness, including the ways in which poorly facilitated reflection could reinforce existing power structures and color-blind statements. Mitchell et al. (2012) argued "reflection on practice must also include a critical lens on race and privilege;" to ignore the potential problems would be to reinforce racist thinking and unequal campus and community relationships (p. 619).

In the same way, to engage students in reflection on leadership experiences without contextual grounding or appropriate reframing of assumptions would be to allow students to codify ways of thinking that reinforce industrial models of leadership and power dynamics that perpetuate injustice. Some steps instructors can implement to facilitate reflection include taking the lead in conversations, introducing topics early in the semester, framing the discussion rather than letting students share feelings devoid of context, and keeping the conversation focused (Mitchell et al., 2012). Additionally, instructors have the responsibility to structure the conversation and model the learning they expect from students when discussing uncomfortable, but important, topics. Considering reflection a necessary tool for engaging the political, Kemmis (1985) noted:

> Reflection is a power we choose to exercise in the analysis and transformation of the situations in which we find ourselves when we pause to reflect. It expresses our agency as the makers of history as well as our awareness that we have been made by it. (p. 149)

Priming students with theory invites deep thinking about society and prepares them for both thought and practice to emancipate structures of injustice.

Taking Action for Justice

For many, questioning assumptions, considering context, and integrating social theory is not enough; critical reflection is also tied to action. Kolb (1984), Mezirow (2000), and others drew from Freire (1970) whose notion of praxis in education called on students to understand the role of identity, power, and privilege in education. As a philosopher who emphasized the close connection between both action and reflection, Freire (1970/1996) coined the term *praxis*:

> But human activity consists of action and reflection: it is praxis; it is transformation of the world. And as praxis, it requires theory to illuminate it. Human activity is theory and practice; it is reflection and action. It cannot ... be reduced to either verbalism or activism. (p. 106)

Freire (1970) rejected notions of change that relied upon oppressors to make concessions to the oppressed; he made a case for education that created space for dialogue, recognizing oppressive forces, and naming the world in order to change systems of oppression. Kemmis (1985) echoed this idea, saying reflection was neither mechanical nor creative, but "it is a practice which expresses our power to reconstitute social life by the way we participate in communication, decisions-making, and social action" (p. 149). The relational elements of reflection and the community connections formed through reflection, with and in communities, create the possibility for action.

We acknowledge many students take action on a regular basis; they may serve at a local nonprofit agency or engage in philanthropy. However, action alone does not rise to the threshold of taking action for justice. Wagner (2017) outlined "four key attributes that distinguish social change from other ways of addressing community problems: is aimed at creating change; addresses the root causes of social problems; is collaborative; [and] is not simple" (pp. 235–236). Can students engage in justice work without understanding the underlying social and political structures? Possibly. But these initiatives, to be inclusive and sustainable, should be anchored in theory and grounded in critical reflection. Wagner (2017) cautioned about possible pitfalls in creating social change. These included assimilation, paternalism, ignoring historical and political contexts, deficit-based approaches, and confusing public relations with social change (Wagner, 2017). Ameliorating a perceived problem without engaging others may seem helpful, but the real work of justice is often complex and involves listening, developing relationships, and demonstrating commitment. Through critical reflection, educators and students should address assumptions about communities, seek assets and allies, and ground their work in context.

In leadership learning, Owen (2016) highlighted opportunities for action. Action is the result of having one's worldview challenged; engaging in dialogue across difference and being exposed to other worldviews; and creating spaces for dialogue with society which "builds solidarity for action" (Owen, 2016, p. 42). Reflection alone is not enough; it must be linked to action. However, as Brookfield (2017) pointed out, there are

risks with critical reflection. Some of the risks are associated with professional practice and competence whereas others are associated with roles
in institutions:

> In colleges and universities, becoming known as a raiser of awkward ques-
> tions can gain you a reputation as a troublemaking subversive who refuses to
> play by the rules that everyone else accepts. Speaking truth to power and
> calling out institutional abuses makes people uncomfortable. (Brookfield,
> 2017, p. 226)

Brookfield (2017) advised it is possible to be aware of and minimize
risks. Although action for justice is often closely aligned with critical social
theory, we intentionally distinguished the two in the continuum because
we acknowledge it may not be possible for people to take desired actions
in their current settings. Along this continuum of critical reflection in
leadership learning, as you move from left to right, the continuum
changes by degree from being more internally focused to looking out-
ward, and from being values and politically neutral to challenging systems
of oppression. We hope that educators will use the term critical reflection
with intentionality and, support students as they question assumptions,
incorporate context, and integrate critical theory for action in their leadership learning process.

CRITICAL REFLECTION IN LEADERSHIP LEARNING

Reflection is significant for leadership learning. As an experiential pedagogy, leadership requires an internal assessment of learning and development through intentional thought. Thompson and Pascal (2012) outlined
two dimensions for critically reflective practice: depth (look beneath surface to see assumptions, thoughts, feelings, and values) and breadth
(broader sociological context including power dynamics and oppression).
Critically reflective leadership learning requires both depth and breadth.
In order to create change, students must become aware of their assumptions and beliefs as well as understand the broader social, political, and
historical contexts in which they are learning and working. The culturally
relevant leadership learning model (Bertrand Jones et al., 2016) codified
the role of identity, capacity, and efficacy in leadership; critical reflection
supports development in these areas. As a social construct deeply influenced by context, identity development—including both social identities
and leader identity—benefits from opportunities for reflection. Although
individual self-reflection supports identity development, Bertrand Jones
et al. (2016) pointed out the significance of relationships in identity development. Through critical reflection, which questions assumptions or inte-

grates critical social theory, students are encouraged to consider the layers of their identity in the context of systems and in preparation for action.

In developing capacity, or the ability to enact leadership, Bertrand Jones et al. (2016) highlighted findings from the Multi-Institutional Study of Leadership (Dugan, Kodama, Correia, & Associates, 2013), which identified high-impact experiences for capacity building. The experiences, which include sociocultural conversations with peers, mentoring relationships, community service, and membership in off-campus organizations (Dugan et al., 2013), include or promote reflection. By applying a critical lens to these reflective conversations, students can be better prepared to understand their identities and develop knowledge, skills, and attitudes for creating positive change.

Perhaps the area where critical reflection has the most potential to benefit leadership learning is through efficacy. Efficacy, the belief in their ability to be successful, is predictive of capacity and highly influenced by contextualized social messages about leadership (Bertrand Jones et al., 2016). Critical reflection that includes critical social theory acknowledges contextual factors and the political nature of reflection. This is significant for bringing about change in spaces where historic and hegemonic structures may negatively influence leadership efficacy, especially for underrepresented students. Reflection plays an important role in leadership learning; specifically, critical reflection supports the development of leadership identity, capacity, and efficacy (Bertrand Jones et al., 2016).

FACILITATING CRITICAL REFLECTION

As we outlined in the continuum of critical reflection, incorporating critical thinking, guiding learners to question assumptions, or integrating critical social theory for action go beyond reflection as an individual tool in service of experiential education. Although confusion over terminology is likely to continue, there is a clear distinction between reflection and critical reflection. Brookfield (2017) acknowledged the time required for critical reflection often makes this an add-on. Specifically looking at teaching, he noted critical reflection can sometimes be employed as a problem-solving process, however, he implored "critical reflection is not a remedial tool; it's a stance of permanent inquiry.... Instead, uncovering assumptions becomes part and parcel of what it means to do good professional work" (Brookfield, 2017, pp. 79–80). Indeed, critical reflection should be used regularly in leadership learning to challenge students to think about complex systems. This section discusses some of the specific ways to incorporate critical reflection in leadership learning.

Scaffolding

In studies where educators attempted to classify student learning, using a variety of rubrics and tools, few students rose to the level of critical reflection (Hatton & Smith, 1995; Kember, McKay, Sinclair, & Wong Yuet, 2008; Ward & McCotter, 2004). Critical thinking is an important component of transformative learning, however, Merriam (2009) wondered about the capability of most adults for this type of learning. Many studies found learners do not reach advanced stages of critical reflection; to this end, how practical is it for most learners to engage in critical reflection? There is not one approach, amount of time, or prompt that leads to critical reflection. Although students are unlikely to think and reflect critically in a short, 5-minute reflection following a 1-hour experiential learning encounter, we cannot say for certain that a specific number of times engaging in experiential learning and reflection will lead to critical reflection. Critical reflection is the result of engagement, support and encouragement from educators, and the willingness of students to engage in complex thinking.

It is clear most students would not be expected to begin with reflection that integrates critical social theory or addresses social issues on a macro scale; however, by engaging students in an iterative process of reflection that moves them from describing experiences to evaluating systems, students can develop knowledge and skills for critical reflection. Critical reflection is not a theoretical aim; it can be practical, but requires investment on the part of educators for their own development as well as the development of their students (Brookfield, 2017; Mitchell et al., 2012).

Coaching and Providing Feedback

Among leadership educators and people who write about reflection, there is strong consensus that critical reflection requires support through mentorship, feedback, or coaching in order for students to engage meaningfully. Although Hatton and Smith (1995) found most students did not reach the highest levels of critical reflection in their written reflection, through analysis, they discovered the importance of a critical friend and the power of reflection with other people. In their early work on reflection, Eyler, Giles, and Schmeide (1996) discussed four "Cs" for reflection—continuous, connected, contextualized, and challenging—and in a later iteration, Eyler and Giles (1999) added a fifth C for coaching. They noted coaching was important for all reflection, particularly for critical reflection, for students to seriously examine assumptions. Liu (2015) affirmed "critical reflection is a complicated social and cognitive process and the habit must be cultivated" (p. 149); in other words, students need educators to support critical reflection through coaching and feedback. In addition to the guiding function of instructors, in learning about leadership, students benefit from critical discourse, which is essential for enhancing understanding and developing empathy (Owen, 2016; Turkle, 2015). For transformative learning to take place, learners benefit from discourse with others and the ability to evaluate their assumptions or gain insights from engagement with others (Mezirow, 2012). The collective experiences of others gleaned through reflective discourse facilitate "critical assessment of assumptions" (Mezirow, 2012, p. 77). As a significant component of leadership learning, relationships are also important for critical reflection. Although referring specifically to transformative learning, Taylor's (2009) assessment of the role of relationships in critical reflection resonates with leadership learning as a relational, cognitive and affective process:

> It is through relationships that learners develop the necessary openness and confidence to deal with learning on an affective level, which is essential for managing the threatening and emotionally charged nature of a transformative learning experience. Without the medium of relationships, critical reflection is impotent and hollow, lacking the genuine discourse necessary for thoughtful and in-depth reflection. (p. 13)

Indeed, Pigza (2015) said "leadership educators at our best are praxis mentors" (p. 47). Through challenging, supporting, and modeling, leadership educators investigate their own beliefs while engaging students in the same process. Holding multiple perspectives at once, leader educators "wade into leadership complexity and remain committed to the cycles of action and reflection necessary for promoting social change in themselves, their students, and the world around us" (Pigza, 2015, p. 47). Critical reflection is unlikely to happen spontaneously; it requires self-development on the part of leadership educators as well as preparation and coaching of students. However, leadership educators who devote the time to facilitating critical reflection may find themselves and their students better positioned to create change and address unjust systems in society.

THERE IS POWER IN COMMUNITY: CRITICALLY REFLECTIVE LEADERSHIP

As leadership is a relational and change-oriented process (Rost, 1993), students will likely encounter situations that require them to think critically and question assumptions. As students work with and in communities, it is important to consider how social, political, and historical contexts inform interactions and privilege certain identities. Through engaging in critical reflection, leaders who take action for justice should undertake true social change efforts (Wagner, 2017) using an asset-based approach (Hamerlinck & Plaut, 2014) in relationship with others. There are multiple ways to engage learners in critical reflection, and developing a broad and deep understanding of self and community requires time and an investment of energy. Critical reflection is more than thinking deeply; it includes confronting biases and questioning assumptions in order to evaluate beliefs. Some students may be drawn to in-depth conversations, some may feel guilty about past uninformed actions, and some may resist conversations that make them uncomfortable. Learners require support to engage in critical reflection (Eyler & Giles, 1999); by challenging students, educators make it possible for students to develop greater understanding of systems and embrace a broader, deeper worldview.

Critical reflection is essential for experiential leadership learning, and the continuum of critical reflection in leadership learning distinguishes some of the nuanced differences between conceptions of critical reflection. Although change processes sometimes spotlight one person as a leader, the real work of change almost always requires investment from many people. Moving along the continuum, each point requires more connection with others. Educators, mentors, and colleagues can support questioning assumptions by asking questions and pointing out blind spots. Considering context can be supported by engaging multiple sources of information about the place you are working. Integrating critical social theory necessitates considering other perspectives and centering marginalized voices. Taking action for justice requires engagement with others—to listen, build relationships, seek feedback, and develop sustainable efforts grounded in real change. In describing reorientation from alternative service trips, Sumka, Porter, and Piacitelli (2015) highlighted how groups of students advocated, planned events to raise awareness, and made long term commitments to organizations. They contrasted the power of collective action and accountability to a group with individual actions: collaborative actions enhance the capacity to create change (Sumka, Porter, & Piacitelli, 2015). Critical reflection in leadership learning creates possibilities for change. Through leadership learning, critical reflection has the opportunity to reclaim its role as a transformative pedagogy and engender action for justice.

CHAPTER 6

BEING A REFLECTIVE
LEADERSHIP EDUCATOR

Many educators incorporate reflection into their practice in both curricular and cocurricular settings. There is evidence to support the cornerstone role of educators and mentors in developing reflective leadership learners (Dugan & Komives, 2007; Dugan, Kodama, Correia, & Associates, 2013). In our survey, when students were asked "How did you learn to reflect?" the most common response was from other people such as family members, friends, mentors, teachers, or counselors. Respondents also identified other people as being important for enhancing reflection. The word education is derived from two Latin words: "*educare* which means to train or to mold, and *educere*, meaning to lead out" (Bass & Good, 2004, p. 162). Bass and Good (2004) pointed out the tension in having two origins, one that implies passing down knowledge through memorization in order to develop good workers, and the other that invokes preparing students for unknown problems through a more active process of thinking, asking questions, and finding solutions. As we described in chapter 2, educational philosophers encourage the latter, favoring active methods of teaching problem solving and reflection over rote memorization (Boud, Keogh, & Walker, 1985a; Dewey, 1933; Freire, 1970/1996; Postman & Weingartner, 1969; Schön, 1983). As we consider the role of reflective educators, we are most interested in educators as facilitators of learning who create opportunities for reflection in order to lead out or draw out students' potential.

Thinking to Transform: Reflection in Leadership Learning
pp. 99–114
Copyright © 2019 by Information Age Publishing
All rights of reproduction in any form reserved.

As we noted in Chapter 4, it is relatively easy to find reflection activities, but perhaps more difficult to consider how activities are mapped to learning outcomes or sequenced as part of a class or program. Reflective educators are familiar with theories that undergird reflection, value the role of reflection in learning, practice reflection, create spaces that invite authentic reflection, and integrate reflection into leadership learning. Although educators are necessary for all elements of the reflection in leadership learning framework, they feature prominently in the support structures. The support structures include people with whom students reflect, feedback, honesty and vulnerability, and time and place for reflection. In this chapter, we elaborate on the significance of reflective leadership educators. We also describe tools for developing as a reflective educator and creating authentic spaces for reflection with students.

REFLECTIVE EDUCATORS AS SUPPORT STRUCTURES

Reflection is often characterized as a solitary activity; however, relationships play a significant role in reflection in leadership learning. Kemmis (1985) pointed out reflection "is not the individualistic working of the mind as either mechanism or speculation; it presumes and prefigures social relationships" (p. 149). Although some learners may reflect deeply without challenge or support, many learners benefit from guidance in the form of facilitated activities, prompts, or feedback. The support structures in the reflection in leadership learning framework (Figure 1.3) highlight the importance of reflective leadership educators. Educators are the people with whom students reflect. They also provide feedback, create spaces that invite honesty and vulnerability, and prioritize time and place for reflection.

In a critical analysis of seven theoretical approaches to reflection in higher education, Rogers (2001) found one of the common factors across approaches to reflection was having a coach or mentor. Students consistently describe the importance of engaging in reflective conversations. In a study of alumni who participated in multiterm community engagement programs during college, Mitchell et al. (2015) found relationships with others were a significant component of reflection. Survey respondents indicated during the time in their civic engagement programs, the most helpful reflection activities were discussion with faculty or advisors and informal dialogue with peers; in their current life, the most helpful reflection activities were dialogue with a partner or close friend or private reflection (Mitchell et al., 2015). Cranton (2006) noted, "Fostering transformative learning in the classroom depends to a large extent on establishing meaningful, genuine relationships with students," and we believe

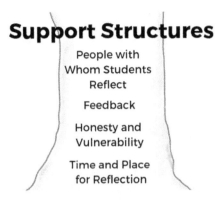

Support Structures

People with
Whom Students
Reflect

Feedback

Honesty and
Vulnerability

Time and Place
for Reflection

FIGURE 1.3. Reflection in leadership learning framework—Support structures.

the same is true for cocurricular learning (p. 5). Through role modeling, facilitating, and teaching others to reflect, educators are a pivotal component of the reflection process.

As part of our survey on reflection in leadership learning, participants were asked "What enhances your reflection?" Students provided a breadth of examples, but two primary categories emerged: being alone and in a quiet place and engaging with other people. Some typical responses related to solitude or quiet included: "Time spent with myself," "A quiet environment," and "Being able to be alone and just think"

Of the respondents who indicated other people enhanced their reflection, some typical responses included:

- "Talking to people in small group settings, or even just talking on the phone with a close friend";
- "Talking it over with several different people who have different ideas and opinions"; and
- "Informal dialogues with fellow peers enhances my ability to ask questions and wrestle with difficult topics."

Some students indicated being alone and with others supported their reflection. One respondent said their reflection was enhanced by, "Being in a secluded place, or in a one on one conversation with someone I can be honest with." These sentiments echo Turkle's (2015) assertion that time alone, with friends, and in society create a "virtuous circle" that supports self-reflection:

In solitude we find ourselves; we prepare ourselves to come to conversation with something to say that is authentic, ours. When we are secure in ourselves, we are able to listen to other people and really hear what they have to say. And then in conversation with other people we become better at inner dialogue. (p. 10)

This also resonates with the dual roles of leadership learning: leader development and leadership development, focusing on the person and the process, respectively. The leadership learning framework (Guthrie & Jenkins, 2018) pointed out the important role of leadership educators in facilitating learning about leadership knowledge, training, development, observation, engagement, and metacognition while also supporting students in reflecting on their knowledge, skills, and values. Educators play a similarly critical role in culturally relevant leadership learning (Bertrand Jones, Guthrie, & Osteen, 2016) through engaging students in reflection on identity, capacity, and efficacy and considering the context for leadership learning. Leadership educators play an important role in facilitating leadership learning, and they can further enhance their capacity by developing knowledge, skills, and attitudes as a reflective leadership educator.

ENHANCING YOUR CAPACITY AS A REFLECTIVE EDUCATOR

Ash and Clayton (2009) asserted instructional designers should be scholars—experimenting, assessing, and refining their work alongside students: "the designer of applied learning opportunities is best understood as a reflective practitioner herself—one who engages in the same critical reflection she expects from her students" (Ash & Clayton, 2009, p. 28). In order to enhance their capacity to integrate reflection into leadership learning, educators should cultivate a reflective practice; simultaneously, educators should develop the skills to guide students through reflection (Johnson, 2009; Molee, Henry, Sessa, & McKinney-Prupis, 2010).

Leadership Educator Identity

Leadership is an interdisciplinary and multidisciplinary field. Leadership educators often come from varying functional areas and academic departments with a variety of past experiences (Guthrie & Jenkins, 2018). Leadership educators may be drawn to the field by facilitating leadership-based programs and workshops or teaching leadership courses in their professional roles (Guthrie & Jenkins, 2018; Seemiller & Priest, 2017). Guthrie and Jenkins (2018) described leadership educators as "all educators who intentionally design and foster leadership development" (p. 19). This includes people in curricular or cocurricular roles and people who have leadership education as the focus of their work or a small portion of the work (Guthrie & Jenkins, 2018). Given the scope of leadership educators, some people may be able to draw from experiential learning or disciplinary knowledge to facilitate reflection, while other leadership educators may not have experience with reflection. Guthrie and Jenkins (2018) encouraged all educators to think about leadership education; to that end, they suggested "developing a personal leadership philosophy and leadership educator philosophy are helpful to consider how the complexities of leadership and identity intersect and emerge personally as a leadership educator" (pp. 19–20). Taking time to reflect and process is vital for educators as they prepare to reflect with students in reflection through challenging conversations.

Research on leadership educators is in the emerging stages. Harding (2011) conducted a phenomenological study of leadership educators' experiences teaching. He found teaching was developmental for many of the educators who explored their identities and made meaning of experience, particularly as part of a learning community of educators (Harding, 2011). Teig (2018) used a case study approach to explore leadership educator preparation of higher education/student affairs master's students. She found a community of practice, created through coursework, internships, assistantships, and influential relationships, supported the development of leadership education identity (Teig, 2018). Identity is at the core of leadership learning makes leadership educator identity development an important area of research and practice (Guthrie & Jenkins, 2018).

To conceptualize the development of leadership educator identity, Seemiller and Priest (2015) drew on literature about professional identity development in the fields of teaching and nursing to create the leadership educator professional identity development model. This model was confirmed through a content analysis of personal narratives from 22 leadership educators who were participants at a national professional development symposium (Seemiller & Priest, 2017). The leadership educator professional identity development model (Seemiller & Priest, 2017) includes four identity spaces through which leadership educators progress: exploration, experimentation, validation, and confirmation. The model includes an element of generativity—after determining if and how they will take on leadership educator identity, and receiving validation from others, they are able to guide other professionals in developing their leadership educator identity (Seemiller & Priest, 2017).

The affirmation of the model was born from educator reflections, and in some ways, elements of this model resonate with the reflection in leadership learning framework. In the study of leadership educators, a pre-exploration phase emerged, and "all 22 participants noted their former leader experiences laid the groundwork for entering into leadership education as a profession" (Seemiller & Priest, 2017, p. 8). The significance of experience coupled with the significance of critical incidents for identity development echoes the role of experience and exposure to leadership theory in the grounding elements of the reflection in leadership learning framework. Other findings from the study—the significance of communities of practice and the important role of mentorship in leadership identity development—mirror the support structure of people with whom students reflect. The generative aspect of the final identity space is similar to the generative elements of the outcomes, particularly the investment in relationships. In this way, the leadership educator professional identity development model (Seemiller & Priest, 2017) underscores the importance of reflection for leadership educators.

Developing a Reflective Practice

When students observe educators reflecting or hear how educators engage in reflection, it may spark curiosity about reflective practice. Role modeling reflection may help with facilitating reflection in the classroom (Ash & Clayton, 2004; Eich, 2008; Guthrie & Jenkins, 2018; Scanlan & Chernomas, 1997). Ash and Clayton (2004, 2009) said it was necessary for faculty to become reflective practitioners in order to serve as models for students and to enhance their capacity to use reflective tools in support of students. Johnson (2009) emphasized the importance of reflection for student affairs practitioners: "daily reflection can lead to better decision-making and critical thinking skills which, in turn, allow student affairs professionals to guide students in more effective ways" (p. 88). To develop as a reflective educator, Scanlan and Chernomas (1997) recommend professionals engage in reflective practices on a regular basis; these can include journaling, meditation, mindfulness or any activity that promotes reflection on experiences. They also encouraged educators to reflect with one another by sharing teaching experiences, asking questions, and offering advice (Scanlan & Chernomas, 1997).

Dyment and O'Connell (2014) recommend the use of journals for people who need structure and routine in their reflective practice. In a study of educators' use of journals, they found participants used journals for organizing deep thoughts, however, many participants rarely reread their journals (Dyment & O'Connell, 2014). Despite this, participants found the process of writing facilitated reflection, and this realization encouraged educators to reconsider how they used journals in the classroom (Dyment & O'Connell, 2014). Different than prescriptive journaling,

Cooper and Stevens (2006) looked at the use of naturalistic journals by higher education professionals. In their journals, professionals captured conversations, developed strategies for managing complex situations, organized their lives, and reflected on their multiple roles (Cooper & Stevens, 2006). Through their reflections, professionals engaged in a metacognitive process of examining the larger picture of their lives (Cooper & Stevens, 2006).

Creating and Holding Space

Educators influence the learning environment in both curricular and cocurricular leadership learning. The culturally relevant leadership learning model (Bertrand Jones et al., 2016) addresses the experiences and backgrounds of marginalized and underrepresented groups in leadership. This model encourages educators to consider how students experience and engage on campus, in the classroom, and in other learning environments (Bertrand Jones at al., 2016). When incorporating reflection, educators need to be aware of the impact of their identities, background, and experiences. Guthrie and Jenkins (2018) described the importance of self-reflection for educators: "we all need to spend time reflecting on how we present ourselves as well as the space we take up in the learning environment" (p. 31). Creating and holding space is a significant component of cultivating reflection. "Holding space" is associated with yoga:

> In yoga, the teacher's task is to hold space for students by providing structure to the class. Although it may seem the teacher holds the power in this interaction, by providing structure, the teacher is actually a tool in the service of the students. (Hikida, 2018, p. 225)

Owen-Smith (2018) identified a tension between how instructors are taught to fill space and making space for mindfulness in the classroom. She described how creating space can be more complementary than contradictory; constructing space "is not to abandon irresponsibly the work of the classroom.... Rather, it is a pause (perhaps just a moment), a breath, and a deepening of presence that allows contemplative practices, as well as classroom methods, to flourish" (p. 56). Burchell and Dyson (2005) described "ways of creating and holding the space for reflection" as part of action research (p. 291). Their strategies included having a flexible structure, creating a culture of finding time for reflection, having opportunities to discuss practice and listen to others, and recognizing how interviewing and facilitation strategies can prompt reflection (Burchell & Dyson, 20015).

In order to empower students, educators need to create learning environments in which both the educator and the student grow and take risks (hooks, 1994). hooks (1994) pointed out when professors expect students to share but are not willing to share themselves, they exercise potentially coercive power. hooks (1994) elaborated on a philosophy: "In my classrooms, I do not expect students to take any risks that I would not take, to share in any way that I would not share" (p. 21). In discussing teaching and learning, Palmer (1998/2007) described the importance of becoming a leader "who opens, rather than occupies, space" which requires "a journey beyond fear and into authentic self-hood, a journey toward respecting otherness and understanding how connected and resourceful we all are" (p. 166). To create and hold space, Guthrie and Jenkins (2018) stressed the importance of educators reflecting deeply on their roles and also taking opportunities to consult with colleagues and mentors regarding pedagogical practices.

Addressing Power Dynamics

Closely related to creating and holding space is the process of uncovering power dynamics. Postindustrial leadership focuses on relationships (Komives et al., 2013: Rost, 1993), and many models of leadership contain a relational element. Building relationships of trust can support and enhance reflection. At the same time, power dynamics persist, particularly in the classroom. Brookfield (2017) described his desire to democratize the classroom and view students as colearners and coteachers; however, he pointed out his naiveté given the "strongly hierarchical culture of higher education, with its structures of authority and its clear demarcation of roles and boundaries" (p. 15). How students understand and relate to authority figures is also influenced by social identities including race, gender, and class, particularly when the instructor identifies differently from the students (Brookfield, 2017).

Mitchell et al. (2012) proposed strategies to interrupt whiteness in service-learning, and recommendations could also contribute to uncovering power dynamics in experiential leadership learning. Mitchell et al. (2012) recommended educators check their assumptions and engage in reflection; they pointed out "It is easy to say that instructions should check assumptions. It is harder to do" (p. 624). They suggested instructors consider students' identities, consciously design experiences for a diverse group of learners, and provide opportunities for students to explore their backgrounds, experiences, and beliefs in the context of experiential learning (Mitchell et al., 2012). One strategy often used to break down barriers and invite discussion is arranging the space in a circle. However, Brookfield (2017) cautioned educators and described the evolution of his teaching practice from arranging the class in a democratic circle to realizing this may make students, particularly students of color or introverted students, feel watched or pressured into engaging in prescribed ways. He noted though he still uses a circle, he explains to students why he uses this format and gives many options for participation so as not to create pressure to perform (Brookfield, 2017). The underlying suggestion for leadership educators is to critically evaluate teaching practices—whether arranging the space, engaging students in discussions about identity, or evaluating reflective work—to uncover structures of power.

Educators who are willing and able to reflect with students may transform experiential leadership learning into a practice of shared learning and meaning making. Mitchell et al. (2012) pointed out the significance of faculty modeling reflection. To enhance the learning community, Ash and Clayton (2004) recommended educators share lessons learned from reflections on their teaching with the classes. Power dynamics exist, regardless of educators' awareness. Brookfield (2017) suggested "authentic collaborations will happen only if teachers spend considerable time earning students' trust by acting democratically, fairly, and respectfully toward them" (p. 15). It is important for educators to uncover power dynamics and progress toward creating spaces that invite reflection from all students.

CREATING SPACE FOR REFLECTIVE LEADERSHIP LEARNING

If reflection is incorporated haphazardly or not facilitated well, it can result in frustration for both facilitators and participants. People who are new to facilitating reflection may think the most important element is having the right activity planned; although activities are important, perhaps more significant is the self-work of developing a reflective practice and becoming comfortable engaging in reflective dialogue which may not always have a clear outcome. In the companion manual, we elaborate on guidelines for facilitation; here, we describe elements that go beyond the essentials for facilitation and include considerations for reflective leadership educators at any point in their professional journey whether in a curricular or cocurricular setting.

Being Open to Emotion

Emotions are an important element of leadership, learning, and reflection, however the role of emotions has not always been clear. Some people perceive reflection is "touchy-feely" or too subjective for the rigor required for evaluative academic work. Additionally, educators "may legitimately fear that they will not be able to adequately or safely address student emotions—or their own emotions" as part of the reflection process (Felten, Gilchrist, & Darby, 2006, p. 43). However, several authors recognized the centrality of feelings or emotions for the process of reflection (Boud et al., 1985; Eyler & Giles, 1999; Moon, 2004). Felten et al. (2006) called attention to Dewey (1933) and Kolb (1984), both of whom cited emotion as a catalyst for thinking, but neither of whom acknowledged the role of emotions in the reflective process. In using the culturally relevant leadership learning model (Bertrand Jones et al., 2016), Mahoney (2017) implored educators to consider affective learning: "Emotions can immobilize, consolidate differences, and reproduce inequality, or emotions can be the barometer for which leadership educators facilitate change and disrupt controlling discourses and ... draw in those on the margins" (p. 59).

Emotional intelligence is a significant concept in leadership popularized by Goleman (1995). Northouse (2016) defined emotional intelligence as "the ability to perceive and express emotions, to use emotions to facilitate thinking, to understand and reason with emotions, and to effectively manage emotions within oneself and in relationships with others" (p. 28). Emotionally intelligent leadership (Shankman, Allen, & Haber-Curran, 2015) is based in emotional intelligence and focuses on consciousness of self, others, and context. Reflection is a central aspect of emotionally intelligent leadership, particularly for developing consciousness of self which "involves awareness of your abilities, emotions, and perceptions" as well as "appreciating that self-awareness is a continual and ongoing process" (p. 10). Moon (2004) argued emotion is central to the reflective process and highlighted multiple ways in which emotions relate to learning and reflection including the influence of emotions on knowledge, the influence of emotions on the process of learning, emotions that may arise from the process of learning, and emotional insights that may arise from reflection. In the context of service-learning, Felten et al. (2006) encouraged educators to "explicitly consider the roles emotion may play throughout the reflection learning process" (p. 42). They pointed out they were not asking for reflection to be reduced to emotion, and acknowledged emotion "always has been, and always will be present" (Felten et al., 2006, pp. 40–41). Including emotion in reflection is not asking educators to be counselors, and educators should be prepared to make referrals for students if necessary. Emotion is a key component of leadership and reflection, and "by ignoring emotions that exist and shape learning, we threaten to shirk our responsibility as educators and to limit potential for real academic learning" (Felten et al., 2006, p. 43).

Encouraging Honesty, Vulnerability, Authenticity

The ability to be honest and vulnerable when reflecting is both signifi-cant and challenging for students. Suskie (2018) noted, "one of the pur-poses of reflective writing is to elicit honest, truthful thoughts from students" (p. 264). However, as we described in Chapters 2 and 4, it can be challenging for students to share authentic reflections, particularly if they are being assessed or they worry their thoughts may not align with educators. Honest reflection also contributes to leadership development. Goleman (1998) highlighted self-awareness as an important element of emotional intelligence, and noted people with strong self-awareness were honest with others and themselves. In order to encourage honest and vul-nerable reflections from students, educators need to clarify the purpose of reflection, create space for genuine reflection, and practice reflection on their own.

Maloney, Tai, Lo, Molloy, and Ilic (2013) explored honesty in summa-tive reflection essays and found 68% of students said they "were at least 80% truthful about their experiences within the reflective essays" (p. 620). In some cases, students were not honest in order to meet assignment cri-teria or because they could not remember an experience. White (2012, 2014) found students understood the significance of reflection in leader-ship learning but struggled to set aside time. When reflection was required for class, students sometimes struggled to elaborate on ideas to meet the required length of an assignment (White, 2012). Helping stu-dents understand the purpose of reflection, including the importance of the process, may enable them to feel more comfortable being honest.

In an examination of leadership learning environments, White and Guthrie (2016) described the pivotal role of instructors in establishing a culture of reflection. One element of encouraging genuine reflection is becoming comfortable with silence when asking questions or facilitating discussion. Silence is important for processing (Moon, 2004). Miller (2005) described the "roller coaster" of rewards and challenges as the "holder of the space" for reflection. The degree to which educators choose to share reflections with students may vary based on comfortabil-ity and context; educators in cocurricular programs may have more lati-tude than instructors. Oftentimes, educators need to take the first step in sharing their reflections; by role modeling self-actualization and vulnera-bility, educators can contribute to a reflective space (hooks, 1994). Although it is not always possible to share reflections with students, whether because it may influence their thoughts or because of the power dynamic between roles, if instructors model reflection and share insights that result from reflective thinking it may enhance their credibility and support students' willingness to share. Finally, as digital spaces become increasingly important for leadership development and students develop a digital leadership identity (Ahlquist, 2017; Stoller, 2013), leadership educators should also consider the role of reflection and vulnerability in online spaces.

Examining Assumptions

Experience alone can be a problematic teacher; some experiences may even serve to reinforce stereotypes (Ash & Clayton, 2009; Jacoby, 2015). Students come to higher education settings with a wealth of experiences and perceptions cultivated throughout their lives. The types of experiences that can prompt reflection—challenging conversations, exposure to thought-provoking literature, or a perplexing incident—may contrast students' beliefs or assumptions. Reflection is important for interrogating beliefs, and educators are especially important for coaching students through critical reflection (Eyler & Giles, 1999; Mitchell et al., 2012; Pigza, 2015).

In discussing how to develop reflective practitioners in teacher education programs, Larrivee (2008) elaborated on three attitudes Dewey (1933) identified as supporting reflective thinking: open-mindedness, whole-heartedness, and responsibility. Dewey (1933) described open-mindedness as being free from things that would prevent someone from considering new perspectives and actively seeking more than one perspective. Larrivee (2008) added open-mindedness includes seeing other points of view as valid rather than treats, shifting from certainty to curiosity, and "being able to let go of needing to be right or wanting to win" (p. 91). Whole-heartedness is demonstrated when someone gives their full attention to something; they are so captivated, they have questions and seek out information (Dewey, 1933). For Dewey (1933), responsibility entailed following through on logical consequences and conclusions, even when they diverged from previously held beliefs. Larrivee (2008) described responsibility as acknowledging impact, foreseen and unforeseen, including positive and negative influences on others. These attitudes may be useful for educators as they examine their assumptions and help students interrogate assumptions.

Students may have assumptions about which they are not aware or that stem from unexamined privilege. The culturally relevant leadership learning model (Bertrand Jones et al., 2016) highlighted the development of leadership identity, capacity, and efficacy taking into account important dimensions of institutional and cultural context. In curricular and cocurricular leadership learning experiences, students may demonstrate varying degrees of awareness of identity. Drawing from a vignette based on service-learning experiences, Mitchell et al. (2012) described the ways in which poorly facilitated reflection can reinforce existing power structures and reinforce color-blind statements. Students may talk about "them" or make statements in their reflections which include generalizations or stereotypes. If faculty and staff are uncomfortable challenging statements that only partially react to an experience or do so in a coded manner, they reinforce beliefs and attitudes based on inaccurate information (Mitchell et al., 2012). The authors pointed out the importance of following up on miseducative statements by asking students "What do you mean by that?" or "How do you know?" and challenging students to think systemically (Mitchell et al., 2012). Uncomfortable or discordant experiences are useful to spark questioning, reflection, and learning, but it is important for educators to provide challenge and support (Sanford, 1967) as students navigate their reflection. Through taking time to reflect and practicing facilitation, educators can become more comfortable facilitating reflection.

Providing Feedback

Stone and Heen (2014) pointed out, "We swim in an ocean of feedback" (p. 1). Feedback is significant for postindustrial leadership which prioritizes collaboration and relationships. Feedback is an important component of students' leadership learning (Boyd & Williams, 2010; Conger, 1992; Komives, Owen, Longerbeam, Mainella, & Osteen, 2005), and it is also an important element in reflection (Hatcher & Bringle, 1997). One of the core tenants of emotionally intelligent leadership (Shankman et al., 2015) is authenticity. Shankman et al. (2015) suggested, "surrounding yourself with peers and mentors who are willing to give you unfiltered and honest feedback will make a difference in your ability to be self-aware" (p. 23). Seeking feedback is only part of the equation; students who seek feedback need to be prepared to manage both positive and critical feedback (Shankman et al., 2015). In addition to providing support for personal growth and helping students deal with specific challenges, an important role for the people who whom students reflect is providing feedback. Feedback supports the reflection process: In a study of reflective blogs kept by graduate students on a month-long international service-learning experience, Sturgill and Motley (2014) found the students whose posts were guided by instructor prompts and feedback were both longer, indicating more time for reflection, and demonstrated higher order thinking.

Giving and receiving feedback is not intuitive. Guthrie and Jenkins (2018) pointed out "to create a culture of feedback, you must provide opportunities for practice" (p. 162). They described the importance of both practice and peer feedback. Similar to the importance of modeling reflection or leadership, educators should model both giving and receiving feedback. Larsen (1998) identified elements of including feedback in the classroom: teaching students about feedback and the feedback process, as well as modeling giving feedback and feedback-seeking behavior. Since opportunities to practice giving and receiving substantive feedback to all students are often limited, Hess (2007) found using a classroom strategy where students lead a team project for 2 weeks and received detailed feedback enhanced their learning and supported greater integration of learning. In order to help students in a management program reflect on feedback, Quinton and Smallbone (2010) gave students written feedback on assignments along with a reflection sheet that asked students how they felt, what they thought, and how they would take action to improve future assignments. Students kept the original reflection and gave a copy to the instructors. Prioritizing time in class for reflection underscored its significance for learning, and also demonstrated the importance of a cycle of assessment, feedback, and reflection on learning (Quinton & Smallbone, 2010). Feedback can be "joined with any active learning strategy," especially those that include a student-facilitated component (Guthrie & Jenkins, 2018, p. 162). Feedback and reflection are closely linked, and educators should prioritize both in curricular and cocurricular settings.

REFRAMING NARRATIVES OF TEACHING AND LEARNING

In Chapter 2, we described the constructivist nature of leadership and reflection, and in chapter 5, we described the importance of critical theory for critical reflection. However, the historically positivist approach to both leadership (Kezar, Carducci, & Contreras-McGavin, 2006) and education (Brookfield, 2017) can make it challenging for educators to engage learners in curricular and cocurricular experiences that are framed by constructivism and critical theory. The lack of alignment with traditionally positivist assessment strategies as well as the practical concerns of how to relate to students through reflection may present challenges. In some ways, we see reflection in leadership learning as an opportunity to challenge existing paradigms and introduce important ways of knowing and being into the classroom and the cocurriculum.

Traditionally, educators have been the keepers of knowledge; however, educators should also consider the knowledge and wisdom that come from students' experiences and reflections. In chapter 2, we discussed how Freire (1970/1996) rejected the "banking" concept of education where students were treated as empty vessels waiting to be filled. Instead, Freire (1970/1996) endorsed "problem-posing" education that does not dichotomize education into teacher and student but "the students—no longer docile learners—are now critical coinvestigators in dialogue with the teachers" (p. 62). Similarly, hooks (1994) focused on teaching as a collaborative process between the teacher and the student. Postman and Weingartner (1969) contrasted metaphors for educators (lamplighters who illuminate minds, gardeners who cultivate minds, muscle builders who strengthen minds, among others) with a focus on meaning making. Although many educational metaphors imply boundaries, a focus on meaning making helps students "learn how to learn" (Postman & Weingartner, 1969, p. 218). Larrivee (2008) observed "preparing reflective practitioners challenges the traditional higher education 'stand and deliver' model, calling for movement away from a trainer perspective toward a learning facilitator and social mediator perspective" (p. 92). Reflective educators must continually examine their assumptions and underlying beliefs; be willing to experience and promote the uncertainty and conflict that prompt learning and reflection; and engage with a friend or peer group who create space for vulnerability and also provide challenge and support (Larrivee, 2008).

Being anchored in constructivist and critical paradigms enables reflection to center ways of learning that may not align with positivist approaches to learning. *Testimonio* (testimony) is derived from the storytelling traditions of Latinx culture. Testimonio can be used as a methodology, a pedagogical tool, or a means of cultivating community with a group of trusted friends or colleagues (Burciaga & Navarro, 2015; Reyes & Curry Rodríguez, 2012). The educational testimonio can be a tool to incorporate reflection into the learning environment. Burciaga and Navarro (2015) defined educational testimonio as an intergenerational process that counters traditional mentorship methods: instead of the mentor directly providing advice and counsel to the mentee, educational testimonio encourages the coconstruction of knowledge and requires the mentor and mentee work closely with one another (Burciaga & Navarro, 2015). Sentipensante pedagogy "represents a teaching and learning approach based on wholeness, harmony, social justice, and liberation" (Rendón, 2009, p. 132). The word sentipensante "comes from a combination of two Spanish words: *sentir*, which means to sense or feel, and *pensar*, to think" (Rendón, 2009, p. 131, emphasis in original). One of the goals of this engaged pedagogy is "to disrupt and transform the entrenched belief system" which requires reflection to address questions about beliefs, power, assumptions, and actions" (Rendón, 2009, p. 135). Sentipensante is transdisciplinary and relationship centered; in the classroom and cocurriculum, it includes engaged learning and invites both emotion and spirituality (Rendón, 2009). It is important for educators to reflect on their assumptions, beliefs, identities, and values, and how these may influence the power dynamic in the learning environment (Brookfield, 2017; Bertrand Jones et al., 2016).

THE HARD AND IMPORTANT WORK OF BECOMING A CRITICALLY REFLECTIVE EDUCATOR

Reflective educators are essential for reflection in leadership learning. Although it is easy to find reflection activities, facilitating curricular and cocurricular experiences that embody reflective leadership learning requires intentional preparation and reflection. In order to facilitate reflection on leadership learning for a diverse group of students, educators need to engage in the important self-work of reflection including examining their own identities, beliefs, and assumptions. Emotionally intelligent leadership is underscored by 10 assumptions about leadership, one of which is "leadership requires inner work" that includes reflection and introspection (Shankman et al., 2015, p. 8). We contend educators need to engage in similar "inner work" in order to develop as reflective practitioners and facilitate reflection with students. Consider how you frame and facilitate reflection. Take the time to develop your reflective practice. Discover what feels intuitive for processing, whether that is writing in a journal, talking to a colleague, walking a labyrinth, or creating an art piece to make meaning of an experience. Practice sharing some pieces of your reflective insights with students, and consider how you hold space for reflection.

Educators fill many functions through role modeling, holding space, acknowledging power dynamics, encouraging honesty, engaging emotions, challenging assumptions, promoting uncertainty, and providing feedback. Engaging students in reflection on leadership learning can be extremely powerful and rewarding; at the same time, Brookfield (2017) acknowledged "becoming critically reflective is hard work, a long incremental haul. In the struggle to do this teachers run political and professional risks and exorcise personal demons" (p. 225). This may be especially true as reflective leadership learning challenges traditional notions of teaching, learning, and scholarship. Colleagues or peers can be important sources of challenge and support. Taking a new approach to something can be risky, but we hope educators consider the potentially powerful impact of changing the narrative of teaching and learning to support reflection in leadership learning.

CHAPTER 7

SEEING THE FOREST
AND THE TREES

Reflection in leadership learning is a dynamic process that supports curricular and cocurricular leadership learning, personal development, and social change. Reflection supports leadership learning through intentional thinking and processing that informs action. Leadership processes catalyze action on what was learned through reflection in order to facilitate positive social change. The reflective leadership learning process supports resilience and is enhanced by mindfulness. Siebert (2005) described how resilience helps people cope with ongoing change or daily pressures; bounce back from difficult experiences; overcome adverse circumstances; and develop new patterns of thinking. A form of contemplative reflection, mindfulness is "an attention to and beholding of our interior selves, a noticing of what is present in that self in the moment" (Owen-Smith, 2018, p. 33). Reflection, leadership, mindfulness, and resilience support the development of leadership identity, capacity, and efficacy (Bertrand Jones, Guthrie, & Osteen, 2016). In this chapter, we explore the significance of resilience and mindfulness for reflection in leadership learning.

Bridges (2016) pointed out "It isn't the changes that do you in; it's the transitions. They aren't the same thing. Change is situational.... Transition, on the other hand, is psychological" (p. 3). Some changes might include starting college, breaking up with a partner, moving, or starting a new job. Although the change may occur relatively quickly, the transition process—which involves letting go of old ways, going through an in-between time or neutral zone, and creating a new beginning—takes time

Thinking to Transform: Reflection in Leadership Learning
pp. 115–134
Copyright © 2019 by Information Age Publishing
All rights of reproduction in any form reserved.

(Bridges, 2016). Whether changes are exciting or painful, anticipated or unanticipated, the journey through the neutral zone can be precarious and also provides opportunities for creativity, renewal, innovation, and developing new patterns (Bridges, 2016). We believe the work of reflection in leadership learning happens in managing the transitions. In this chapter, we use the word change to encompass the full process of change and transition. We close with an examination of broader community impacts of resilience and reflection in leadership learning.

CHANGE: A COMMON AIM OF LEADERSHIP AND REFLECTION

Change is at the heart of both reflection and leadership. In describing a postindustrial model of leadership, Rost (1993) defined leadership as "*an influence relationship among leaders and followers who intend real changes that reflect their mutual purposes*" (p. 102, emphasis in original). Kotter (2012) laid out an eight-step process for facilitating change. Quinn (1996) discussed deep change as change that goes beyond incremental differences to develop new ways of being. At the hub of the social change model (Higher Education Research Institute, 1996), change "does not refer to simple, surface-level shifts but to the complex changes that require examination of our individual and collective ways of being" (Wagner, 2017, pp. 203–204). Wheatley (2006) drew on chaos theory to inform challenges for how organizations operate and new complex ways of being. Heifetz and Linsky (2002) distinguished technical challenges (which utilize current knowledge) from adaptive challenges (which require learning new ways) and described the risk associated with adaptive changes: "The deeper the change and the greater the amount of new learning required, the more resistance there will be and, thus, the greater danger to those who lead" (p. 14). The list could go on, but it is clear leadership is concerned with change.

The transformation that results from change is central to reflection. Philosophers and educational theorists described an iterative process that included both action and reflection (Dewey, 1933; Kolb, 1984; Mezirow, 1978a, 2012; Schön, 1983). Rogers (2001) pointed out "a final step in most models of reflection is taking action based on the reflective process" (p. 45). As a result of reflection, learners may gain insight that prompts an evaluation of assumptions, beliefs, or values (Mezirow, 1978a, 2012). One of the powerful aspects of reflection in leadership learning is the possibility for collective learning and movement for positive social change. Sumka, Porter, and Piacitelli (2015) described this collective change through the lens of reorientation from sustained experiential service trips also known as alternative breaks. Reorientation builds on experiences and lessons learned through reflection; it can take many forms including "local community engagement and service, political advocacy, changes in daily life choices, commitment to philanthropy, a chance in academic major, organizing others for change, or a shift in career path" (Sumka et al., 2015, p. 167). Although individual changes are significant, "there is a greater opportunity for change through organizing and unifying all these enlightened individuals into a productive movement of people working collectively to address some of the social and environmental challenges of our time" (Sumka et al., 2015, p. 170). When developed with communities using a critical social theory lens, the intersection of service-learning and leadership provides rich opportunities for learning through reflection and sustainable community change (Owen, 2016; Wagner & Pigza, 2016).

It is important for leaders to be adaptable and comfortable with change (Bandura, 1998; Heifetz, 1991; Heifetz & Linsky, 2002). As Bridges (2016) pointed out, change is fast, but transition takes time. Between the end of one thing and the beginning of the next is a neutral zone (Bridges, 2016). Bridges (2016) described the neutral zone as entering "a state of affairs in which neither the old ways nor the new ways work satisfactorily;" depending upon the depth and breadth of the change, the neutral zone could last for weeks, months, or years (p. 45). Although the neutral zone can generate anxiety, reduce productivity, or uncover weakness, with patience, strategy, and reflection, it can also be a time to encourage creativity, experimentation, and innovation (Bridges, 2016). Siebert (2005) described resilience as an action and or reaction to change. How a person copes with change, navigates change, and processes change are indicative of their level of resilience. Highly resilient people are flexible, adapt to new circumstances quickly, and thrive through change (Siebert, 2005). Resilience and mindfulness are important concepts connected to reflective leadership learning.

SURVIVING AND THRIVING THROUGH RESILIENCE

Resilience is salient to many fields including engineering, psychology, and environmental science. In engineering, resilience describes a mechanical behavior of materials when exposed to force or load (Campbell, 2008). Specifically, resilience "is the ability of a metal to absorb energy when elastically deformed and then to return it when it is unloaded" (Campbell, 2008, p. 206). When used colloquially to describe people, resilience is the ability to bounce back from hard times. In a broader environmental sense, resilience thinking is "about how periods of gradual changes interact with abrupt changes, and the capacity of people, communities, societies, and cultures to adapt or even transform into new development pathways in the face of dynamic change" (Folke, 2016, p. 2). Resilience has recently become a focus in higher education. One multi-institutional study focused on the transition to college for first-year students found "stress is highly prevalent among college freshman, and students often engage in maladaptive behaviors in response to stress," however, regardless of their stress level resilience promoted "positive mental and emotional well-being for students during the transition to college" (DeRosier, Frank, Schwartz, & Leary, 2013, p. 542). Resilience is an important concept not just for individuals, but for groups, communities, and society.

Grotberg (2003b) noted resilience is important for all people: "Resilience is the human capacity to deal with, overcome, learn from, or even be transformed by the inevitable adversities of life" (p. 1). Although all people experience adversity, the way people perceive and experience adversity varies (Grotberg, 2003b). Reivich and Shatté (2002) described three reactive uses for resilience: overcoming negative circumstances of childhood, navigating chronic stress (such as arguments, running late, or an unexpected expense), and bouncing back from a traumatic experience. Resilience neither stems the tide of stressors nor protects people from stressors, but it can be developed in order to deal with stressful events and information (Grotberg, 2003b).

Richardson (2002) outlined three waves of research on resilience. The first wave used phenomenological inquiry to uncover characteristics or traits of people that allowed them to overcome adversity (Richardson, 2002). The study of resilient qualities took shape in the mid 1900s and represented a paradigm shift from examining risk factors to understanding strengths and protective factors for psychosocial problems (Reivich & Shatté, 2002; Richardson, 2002). Early researchers began investigating "children who came out of a highly stressed environment and yet seemed to be very adaptive" (Rolf & Glantz, 2002, p. 6). Stressors could be significant events, and they could also be an accumulation of many daily stressors (Rolf & Glantz, 2002). The second wave of research moved to looking at resiliency as a process for "coping with stressors, adversity, change, or opportunity in a manner that results in the identification, fortification, and enrichment of protective factors" (Richardson, 2002, p. 308). This shifted resiliency beyond the ability to bounce back and toward a process of growth through disruptive experiences (Richardson, 2002). The third wave focused on resilience theory: "there is a force within everyone that drives them to seek self-actualization, altruism, wisdom, and harmony with a spiritual source of strength" (Richardson, 2002, p. 313). This interdisciplinary, postmodern view situates resilience theory as a motivational force for the intentional utilization of strength for the individual or group (Richardson, 2002); beyond bouncing back or reintegrating new insights, resilience theory suggests a more integrated, relational, and holistic approach to development.

Reflection is closely connected to resilience. Coutu (2002) linked resilience to both meaning making and sensemaking. Other scholars highlighted the work of Austrian psychiatrist and Holocaust survivor Viktor Frankl (1946) who wrote about meaning making in the face of unimaginable adversity (Reivich & Shatté, 2002; Siebert, 2005). Resilience is an important tool for managing challenges, but it goes beyond dealing with adverse circumstances. Developing resilience may also contribute to living life fully or reaching goals (Grotberg, 2003b; Richardson, 2002). Reivich and Shatté (2002) identified resilience as a proactive capacity; the reaching out function of resilience includes assessing risks, becoming comfortable with expressing ideas, and finding meaning and purpose in experiences. They said finding meaning in life "requires a focus on the here and now, a mindfulness that many of us lack, coupled with the ability to see the big picture" (Reivich & Shatté, 2002, p. 29). Mindfulness is an important component of reflection that supports resilience and leadership.

CONTEMPLATIVE PRACTICE, MINDFULNESS, AND THE POWER OF PRESENCE

Though many people may associate contemplative practices with a religious or spiritual tradition, these practices are also connected to intellectual inquiry (Barbezat & Bush, 2014). Anchored in experiential learning, contemplative practices invite learners to shift from a purely cerebral understanding of material to a more personal and integrated application that cements learning through experience and connection with others (Barbezat & Bush, 2014). Contemplative pedagogy "uses forms of introspection and reflection that allow students to focus internally and find more of themselves in their courses" (Barbezat & Bush, 2014, p. 9). The Center for Contemplative Mind in Society (2014) developed the tree of contemplative practices (Figure 7.1) which outlines many contemplative practices; although not an exhaustive list, it highlights the breadth of practices. In our survey of reflection in leadership learning, students described contemplative practices or settings that fostered reflection. In response to the prompt "What enhances your reflection?" the most frequent answers included silence, quiet, alone, calm environment, and clear or peaceful mind. Respondents described contemplative practices including music, yoga, journaling, and meditation. Some of the learning objectives connected to contemplative practices may include focus and attention, deeper understanding of course material, compassion and con-

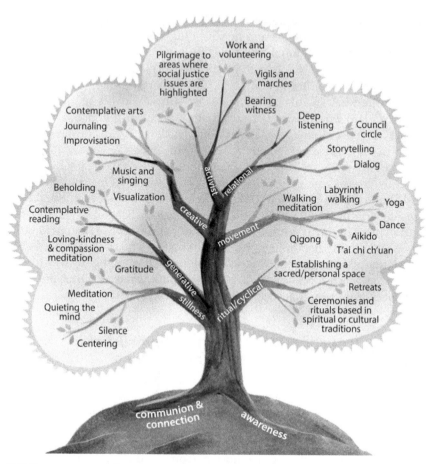

FIGURE 7.1.   Tree of contemplative practices. Reprinted with permission from http://www.contemplativemind.org/practices/tree. Copyright 2014 by The Center for Contemplative Mind in Society.

nection, and personal inquiry (Barbezat & Bush, 2014). It is important to note including contemplative practices in learning is not about imposing the views of a particular religious or spiritual tradition, but engaging students in exploring and investigating their beliefs and values (Barbezat & Bush, 2014).

Contemplative reflection is a complement to leadership learning; many of the core values or qualities associated with contemplative practice align with knowledge, skills, and values for leadership development. The Center for Contemplative Mind in Society (2018) identified core values or qualities for contemplative practice as patience, wisdom, honest self-reflection, calmness, integrity in the midst of complex situations, compassion, focus, skillful listening and community, and creativity. As a relational process focused on change, leadership requires many of the same skills such as integrity, self-reflection, skillful listening, and creativity, among others. Many leadership programs include contemplative practices including retreats, dialogue circles, storytelling, or improvisation (Guthrie & Jenkins, 2018). Similar to reflection and leadership, contemplative methods go beyond individual benefit: "Personal introspection and contemplation reveal our inextricable connection to each other, opening the heart and mind to true community, deeper insight, sustainable living, and a more just society" (Barbezat & Bush, 2014, p. xv). Although there are many forms of contemplative reflection, we focus on mindfulness and its role in resilience and reflective leadership.

Mindfulness

Although many contemplative practices are methods for reflection, mindfulness has received significant attention as a practice that supports the development of resilience and leadership. The concept of mindfulness was introduced to Western culture by a Vietnamese monk, Thich Nhat Hanh, who engaged in mindfulness and Buddhist practices toward peaceful social change (Webster-Wright, 2013). Mindfulness is "both a process (mindfulness practice) and an outcome (mindful awareness)" (Barbezat & Bush, 2014, p. 95). It may be thought of "as a state of consciousness, one characterized by attention to the present experience with a stance of open curiosity" (Smalley & Winston, 2010). Broadly speaking, technological advances have created incredible opportunities for society, but the proliferation of technology and the availability of information may have come at the expense of mental and emotional well-being (Smalley & Winston, 2010). As society reconciles technological advances with associated costs, attention has returned to the ancient practice of mindfulness (Smalley & Winston, 2010).

In an interview, Dr. Zabat-Kinn, founding executive director of the Center for Mindfulness in Medicine, Health Care, and Society at the University of Massachusetts Medical School, described mindfulness operationally as "moment-to-moment, nonjudgmental awareness. It is cultivated attention in a particular way, namely, on purpose in the present moment—and I emphasize, nonjudgmentally" (Gazella, 2005, p. 60). Webster-Wright (2013) argued for the importance of mindfulness in everyday lives. She conceptualized "mindful inquiry" as an interplay between the calm, receptive space of mindfulness and the questioning, probing space of inquiry; the in between space allows for exploring uncertainty, doubt, or insight (Webster-Wright, 2013).

Mindfulness practices have been used to promote the development of awareness and the ability to navigate emotions. In an exploratory case study of an adventure-based learning trip to Sequoia National Park, Stuhr, Lecomte, and Sutherland (2017) found participants experienced "friendship (social connection and social support) and mindfulness (reflective awareness and serenity)" (p. 410). By traveling away from a suburban setting and leaving behind technology, participants were able to "be in the moment and pay closer attention to their own thoughts and interactions with others" (Stuhr et al., 2017, p. 415). A study of first-year students who participated in a mindful communication seminar found students benefited from meditation, and mindfulness practice may support emotional regulation and a mind-body connection that facilitates mindful health choices (Ramasubramanian, 2017). A study of a mindfulness experiential small group to develop counselors-in-training found mindfulness "may assist counselors-in-training to successfully navigate difficult emotions and tolerate ambiguity that are a part of learning" while also providing skills that could be used in clinical practice (Bohecker, Vereen, Wells, & Wathen, 2016, p. 28). For a group of healthcare practitioners, mindfulness and reflection using poetry surfaced discomfort and uncertainty; paradoxically, sitting with these emotions may facilitate awareness, resiliency, and connection with others (Nugent, Moss, Barnes, & Wilks, 2011). Although mindfulness is rooted in Buddhism (Webster-Wright, 2013), educators can use mindfulness practices in a secular setting (Barbezat & Bush, 2014).

MINDFULNESS AND RESILIENCE
IN A DISTRACTED, CHAOTIC WORLD

Our current reality is a double-edged sword: for many people, the wealth of information available at their fingertips through a smart phone, tablet, or laptop is unprecedented. At the same time, our increased reliance on technology to not only meet but anticipate our needs may also be creating a gap in our ability to be present and develop relationships. A recent experimental study that employed objective behavioral coding found the presence of smartphones reduced smiling in casual social interactions (Kostadin, Hunter, Proulx, Pressman, & Dunn, 2019). Another study of conversational dyads found evidence that "the mere presence of mobile phones inhibited the development of interpersonal closeness and trust, and reduced the extent to which individuals felt empathy and understanding from their partners" (Przybylski & Weinstein, 2012, p. 244). In one survey, the Pew Research Center (2018b) found "smartphone owner-ship has become a nearly ubiquitous element of life: 95% of teens now report they have a smartphone or access to one" and "45% of teens now say they are online on a near-constant basis" (p. 2). Teens, who represent the next wave of collegegoers, near constant use of technology coupled with pervasive use of social media platforms begs the question of how educators can use these tools for positive educational benefits?

On the other hand, in another survey the Pew Research Center (2018a) found social media was an influential tool for advocacy and activism: of those surveyed, the majority agreed social media was a powerful tool for getting elected officials to listen, sustaining momentum, and giving voice to underrepresented groups. This is not a simple question of whether technology is "good" or "bad"; it is important to consider the nuanced role of technology in our lives and how to manage the potentially disrup-tive impacts on relationship development and the ability to be present. Our constant need to be engaged and productive may also be owed to an educational system where "the stillness and quiet necessary for thought development and deep intellectual inquiry become nonproductive, a wasting of time, and a squandering of resources" (Owen-Smith, 2018, p. 2). Notions of productivity and connectedness through technology are competing for the limited bandwidth of attention.

At the same time as we navigate both digital and in-person relation-ships, we are negotiating significant environmental and human-made challenges. Resiliency is important for day-to-day stressors, personal trag-edies, and national or global events. Although published over 15 years ago, Grotberg's (2003a) words resonate today:

> There may be as many disasters today as ever. There may be as many trage-dies, killings, riots, snipers, and criminals as ever. But today we learn about them, see them on television, read about them in the papers and journals, and are bombarded with news of them. The result is we experience more stress than ever before with a constant barrage of bad news. (p. ix)

It is debatable whether there are more environmental and human-created disasters today than there were 15, 50, or 100 years ago; what is clear is the rate at which we receive information has drastically acceler-ated. Smart phones and social media have enabled the sharing of infor-mation in real time. Although potentially advantageous for activism and advocacy, the rate at which we learn of national and global disasters, injus-tice, and political unrest can have the effect of feeling like being pum-meled by waves in the ocean: as soon as one wave passes, the next is cresting on the horizon. We frame this not to create a sense of hopeless-ness, but to contextualize the significance of developing resilient and mindful leaders who engage in an inclusive, critical, and reflective leadership process.

RESILIENT, MINDFUL, REFLECTIVE LEADERSHIP

If we were to imagine a concept map with reflection, leadership, resilience, and mindfulness, there would be many connectors to show how these concepts exist in an interconnected web. Reviewing the core tenants of each concept, there are several common elements that facilitate resilient, mindful, reflective leadership learning: they can be developed; identity, self-awareness, and emotion are central; and mentors play a role in facilitating development. To begin, we describe how these concepts are underscored and advanced by having a growth mindset.

Supported by a Growth Mindset

Growth mindset "is based on the belief that your basic qualities are things you can cultivate through your efforts, your strategies, and help from others" (Dweck, 2016, p. 7). Our mindset is our established set of attitudes, which profoundly influences the way we live and how we navigate decisions. In 2006, Dweck introduced two types of mindsets: fixed and growth. People with a fixed mindset believe the qualities they possess will not change, and are, in fact, set (Dweck, 2006). Individuals with a fixed mindset feel the need to prove themselves constantly to show their intelligence, personality, and moral character are enough (Dweck, 2006). People with a growth mindset believe through efforts, strategies, and support from others, their basic qualities can be cultivated, and they are able to grow (Dweck, 2006). Individuals with a growth mindset tend to achieve more than those with a fixed mindset (Dweck, 2016).

People do not have either a fixed mindset or a growth mindset: "Everyone is actually a mixture of fixed and growth mindsets, and that mixture continually evolves with experience" (Dweck, 2016, para. 4). How this mixture shows up will vary based on context, situation, and experience. Mindset development is complex and includes messages received in the past, personal histories of success and failure, and how people responded to these outcomes (Duckworth, 2016). For example, was someone praised for natural talent or working hard? Did people in authority respond to failure or success in ways that affirmed growth or inability to improve? Dweck (2016) cautioned some individuals have a false growth mindset. They confuse having a growth mindset with being flexible, open-minded, or simply having a positive outlook (Dweck, 2016). Some individuals believe they have always possessed growth mindset qualities and there is no need to work toward improvement.

Possessing a growth mindset is more complex than believing you have one. It is essential to intentionally choose a growth mindset, but it also requires continual reflection to seek enlightenment around personal improvement. Individuals with a growth mindset defined success as doing their best, especially when they were learning and improving (Dweck, 2006). They found setbacks informative, took charge of processes that brought them success, and maintained successful processes. Cultivating and attaining a growth mindset is hard work because we all have things that prompt fixed mindset behaviors. Whether facing challenges, receiving criticism, or comparing ourselves with others, we all have insecurities, which inhibit growth (Dweck, 2016). To continue to be in a growth mindset, we must acknowledge triggers and deepen our understanding of growth mindset concepts and processes.

Supporting Growth Mindset in Others

Growth mindset is not only how we lead our lives, but also how we interact with and lead others. Dweck (2006) drew the distinction between the actions of leaders with a fixed mindset versus a growth mindset. Fixed mindset leaders believe some people are superior and others are inferior, which mirrors fixed mindset individuals. Leaders with a fixed mindset must repeatedly affirm they are superior. However, leaders with a growth mindset believe that leadership is about growth and passion. Dweck (2006) pointed out growth-minded leaders displayed gratitude and constantly acknowledged those who were engaged with them in the process of leadership made the journey possible.

A common misconception of developing growth mindsets in others is that praising and rewarding effort is enough (Dweck, 2006). Outcomes matter in work, school, and working toward a goal. As a leader with a growth mindset, although it is critical to reward effort, learning, and progress, it is also important to highlight help-seeking behaviors that support the process of reaching the outcome. To support a growth mindset in others, leaders should both embody and espouse a growth mindset. Duckworth (2016) stated this beautifully: "Language is one way to cultivate hope. But modeling a growth mindset—demonstrating by our actions that we truly believe people can learn to learn may be even more important" (p. 182). Leaders can encourage growth mindset by encouraging appropriate risk-taking, understanding some risks will not work out as planned, and supporting followers as they learn (Dweck, 2016).

A complete, pure growth mindset does not exist; rather, individuals need to seek improvement to continually enhance their capacity for a growth mindset, and reflection is essential to this process. Growth mindset "leads to a desire to learn and therefore a tendency to embrace challenges, persist in the face of setbacks, see effort as a path to mastery, learn from criticism, [and] find lessons and inspiration in the success of others" (Dweck, 2006, p. 263). As metacognition underscored the development of critical reflection, growth mindset underscores resilience and mindfulness as key complements to reflection in leadership learning. Embracing a growth mindset enables learners to explore complexity, deal with adversity, embrace presence, and engage in the change process. As we explore elements of resilient, mindful, and reflective leadership, we understand the importance of a learning orientation and a growth mindset for individual, group, and community development.

Developed Through Experience

Both leadership and resilience were once thought of as trait-based phenomena, but through experience and research, it is clear both leadership and resilience can be developed (Dugan, 2017; Grotberg, 2003b; Richardson, 2002). Grotberg (2003b) dispelled the notion that resilience is a "quality only a few lucky people have" and noted resilience can be promoted in children, youth, and adults (p. 3). Guthrie and Jenkins (2018) outlined elements of leadership learning that enable learners to engage in the process of leadership and develop as leaders. In fact, leadership and resilience may be developed in tandem: Conger (2004) recognized hardships as one of many factors that shape the development of leaders. Grotberg (2003b) identified factors (as opposed to traits or characteristics) that promote resilience: external supports ("I have"), inner strengths ("I am"), and interpersonal, problem solving skills ("I can"). She noted many people have developed these factors, but they may be more difficult to deploy in new or unfamiliar situations (Grotberg, 2003b). Similarly, both reflection and mindfulness can be cultivated. Mindfulness is both a state of consciousness as well as a quality of attention; it can be cultivated through explicit practices or by adopting a mindful approach (Smalley & Winston, 2010). Reflection is an iterative process that can be learned and also promotes learning. Through experiential learning, it may be possible to concurrently develop knowledge, skills, and attitudes for leadership, resilience, mindfulness, and reflection.

One avenue for developing resilience is through outdoor orientation programs (Baruch & Stutman, 2003; Hill, Posey, Gomez, & Shapiro, 2018) or outdoor leadership programs (Overholt & Ewert, 2015). These programs provide opportunities for students to overcome difficulties, which may "foster the resilience that college students need to cope successfully with a new setting, new rules, new demands, and new stresses" (Baruch & Stutman, 2004, p. 43). Adventure-based learning can also develop mindfulness and reflection (Stuhr et al., 2018). Course-based experiences may also promote development. By incorporating tenants of positive psychology and high-impact practices into an experiential learning course that was supported by both student affairs and academic affairs, Mahatmya, Thurston, and Lynch (2018) found "promising findings, especially regarding the potential to enhance mindfulness, resilience, and social connectedness in undergraduate students through a course that explicitly deals with the academic and experiential dimensions of the science of well-being" (p. 303). In a study of student leadership development, Wolf Williams and Allen (2015) found traumatic experiences can sometimes prompt engagement in prosocial causes, and resilience may be a factor which supports engagement with a cause related to the experience. Although resilience, leadership, mindfulness, and reflection may be the focus of individual programs or courses, developing these in tandem may be a powerful means to support learning and growth.

Identity, Self-Awareness, and Emotion Are Central Elements

Identity and self-awareness are significant aspects of leadership, reflection, resilience, and mindfulness. As a relational process, identity and understanding the intersectional layers of identity are at the heart of leadership (Bertrand Jones et al., 2016). Identity development is supported through reflection which includes self-assessment (Bertrand Jones et al., 2016). Resilience is also supported by increasing self-awareness (Christman & McClellen, 2012; Reivich & Shatté, 2002; Howard & Irving, 2014). Reivich and Shatté (2002) identified seven skills that support resilience, and three of those skills are connected to emotion and self-awareness: emotional regulation and staying calm under pressure, empathy, and self-efficacy or sense of effectiveness in the world. Emotional consciousness of self is a key construct in a multitude of models and theories in leadership education curriculum (Allen, Shankman, & Miguel, 2012; Shankman, Allen, & Haber-Curran, 2015). As leaders grow in their emotional intelligence, grasping more deeply their authentic sense of self in relationship to others, they can also intensify their capacity for resilience (Allen et al., 2012; Howard & Irving, 2014; Shankman et al., 2015). Implementing an intentional reflective practice facilitates growth in a leader's depth of understanding about themselves (self-awareness) and in relationship to others (consciousness of others) (Shankman et al., 2015). Leadership development provides a means to connect self-awareness and identity development in order to foster resilience.

Mindfulness is significant for self-development and enhancing relationships. Practicing mindfulness and developing a nonjudgmental awareness of the present moment may facilitate self-understanding (Barbezat & Bush, 2014) or increased awareness of thoughts and emotions (Smalley & Winston, 2010). Mindfulness may also support the development of emotionally intelligent leadership (Shankman et al., 2015) through increasing empathy, understanding others' emotions, regulating emotions, valuing other perspectives, and forming relationships (Lucas, 2015). Howard and Irving (2014) contended greater self-awareness and sense of identity were developed through hardships and supported the development of resiliency. They argued "among other factors self-awareness and identity are shaped in hardships and obstacles early on in an individual's life" and these obstacles served as precursors to leadership development (Howard & Irving, 2014, p. 472). Christman and McClellen (2012) noted, "resiliency develops and substantiates self-awareness and identity. As individuals encounter adversity, they navigate potential responses—to fight or flee. These experiences and self-awareness contribute to the construction of identity" (p. 651). They argued that, similarly, "leadership rests upon the development of self-awareness and identity" and therefore "understanding how leaders define and describe their resiliency tells us how they attempt to identify themselves" (Christman & McClellen, 2012, p. 651).

The culturally relevant leadership learning model (Bertrand Jones et al., 2016) demonstrated the importance of contextualizing leadership development. By intentionally considering domains of organizational and campus culture, we can understand the differential impact of the campus context on students from diverse backgrounds and identities. It is similarly important to consider the contextual factors that lead to the development of resilience. Patton, Renn, Guido, and Quaye (2016) described how privilege and oppression impact social identity development, including resilience: "Under certain conditions the interaction of minority stress and negative campus climate might become a catalyst for the development of agency and resilience, but it also could easily impede student development, learning, and success" (p. 77). It is important to consider the development of resilience across and at the intersection of social identities including gender, race, class, and sexual orientation, among others. Grounded in critical theory, Yosso's (2005) community cultural wealth model serves as an asset-based framework for what students of color bring to their lived experiences. Community cultural wealth model (Yosso, 2005) includes six types of capital, and both aspirational capital and navigational capital connect to resilience. Aspirational capital "refers to the ability to maintain hopes and dreams for the future, even in the face of real and perceived barriers" (Yosso, 2005, p. 78). Navigational capital refers to steering through social institutions, and the ability of students to persist despite spaces that may be hostile to people of color or stressful events in the environment. Both of these forms of capital, in the context of the community cultural wealth model (Yosso, 2005) provide examples of how students of color develop resilience. Identity is a central element of resilience and leadership, and the development of identity is facilitated by reflection and mindfulness.

Supported by Mentors

Mentorship is a key component for developing leadership, reflection, resilience, and mindfulness. Leadership educators serve important roles in the leadership learning process including developing outcomes and curriculum, facilitating curricular and cocurricular experiences, providing feedback, assessing learning, and overall creating learning communities (Guthrie & Jenkins, 2018). Educators are also essential for facilitating and modeling reflection including prompting questions, challenging assumptions, and providing feedback (Eyler & Giles, 1999; Mitchell et al., 2012; Pigza, 2015). Lucas (2015) emphasized that modeling mindfulness in curricular and cocurricular settings was just as important as teaching students about mindfulness. To better support students with multiple intersectional identities, it is important for faculty and staff to understand context including bias, discrimination, and inequalities (Ward, 2018). It is only with this understanding that educators can help shift students from resistance, a psychological survival strategy of resisting negative social influences, to resilience and the ability to positively adapt through adversity (Ward, 2018). Resilience is driven by context, and mentors need to acknowledge any approach that does not acknowledge multiple intersecting identities may exclude some students (Ward, 2018).

In reflection and leadership learning, educators balance challenge and support (Sanford, 1967). Educators fulfill a similar function in promoting resilience. Baruch and Stutman (2003) described how staff at the Institutes for Mental Health Initiatives determined two significant, and somewhat paradoxical, elements of resilience. The first was mentorship, or "the love, the devotion, and care of at least one person in a child's life" (Baruch & Stutman, 2003, p. 31). The second included "small exposures to adversity" where "although anxiety will be aroused, mastery of the challenge is assured" (Baruch & Stutman, 2003, p. 41). Reflective and experiential leadership learning provides opportunities for students to develop resiliency. Through curricular and cocurricular experiences, educators frame circumstances that provide sufficient challenge for the developmental stage of the students. Reflection is particularly significant for challenging experiences as it allows students to vent frustrations and receive feedback which may inform alternate interpretations of a situation. By developing spaces where students feel safe to share authentically and process challenging experiences, educators can support the development of resiliency and leadership.

Parks Daloz, Keen, Keen, and Daloz Parks (1996) described the significance of mentors for development. As people who "challenge, support, and inspire," mentors "function as compelling women and men who recognize and support the emerging competence of the young adult, challenge limited notions of possibility, and offer themselves as beacons toward significance purpose" (pp. 44–45). Mentors can take many forms including family members, coaches, instructors, supervisors, or other figures who have experience that a mentee is drawn toward (Parks Daloz et al., 1996). Johnson, Taasoobshirazi, Kestler, and Cordova (2015) studied the impact of "models of resilience (those who demonstrate persistence on challenging tasks)" and "messengers of resilience (those who offer words of encouragement, like 'you can do this!')" on students' perceived resilience and use of regulatory strategies for academic success (p. 869). They found models of resilience were important for students perceived resilience and noted, "when a learner identifies strongly with a model who persists in the face of challenges/adversity, the learner's self-efficacy to persist on similar tasks/challenges can endure" (Johnson et al., 2015, p. 880). Although both had positive effects, they found models of resilience had a stronger direct influence than messengers and suggested students gain "vicarious experiences by interacting with positive models of resilience" (Johnson et al., 2015, p. 880). When focusing on the development of resilient, mindful, and reflective leaders, the models of resilience need to reflect the identities of the students. Equally as important as mentors or models are mentoring environments. Mentoring environments may include mentors, colleagues, or friends who are facing similar challenges or experiences as well as resources that may include knowledge, time, or technical training (Parks Daloz et al., 1996). Developing resiliency and mindfulness for reflective leadership learning requires a community of people to offer challenge and support.

REFLECTIVE LEADERSHIP FOR THRIVING COMMUNITIES

Grotberg (2003b) noted, "Everyone can become resilient. The challenge is to find ways to promote it in individuals, in families, and in communities" (p. 3). A key element of this statement is the importance of community resilience. Resilience has been critiqued for focusing on the individual without consideration of structural forces (Collins, 2017). This point is underscored by Parks Daloz et al. (1996) who conducted interviews with over 100 people who "sustained long-term commitments to work on behalf of the common good, even in the face of global complexity, diversity, and ambiguity" (p. 5). To frame an examination of the common good, they began by contrasting a "legacy of individualism" which includes individual "armor" such as busyness, consumerism, cynicism, and tribalism (Parks Daloz et al., 1996). This turn toward the individual reduces contemplation of complex problems and recuses people of a responsibility to support one another. However, similar to both reflection and leadership, a focus on community resilience that supports the common good may create possibilities for systemic change.

In planning for resilient communities, architects and urban planners consider the built environment and support systems. The built environment includes physical structures and how they are organized at different levels from city block to region (Coyle, 2011). Support systems for the built environment include transportation, energy, water, natural environment, food production/agriculture, solid waste, and economic (Coyle, 2011). Sustainable and resilient communities are walkable or drivable and include structures that can adapt to serve multiple functions to meet economic or societal needs (Coyle, 2011). In contrast, at risk communities are only accessible by automobile and include single-use subdivisions or strip malls that are not easily repurposed (Coyle, 2011).

At the macrolevel, communities encounter large-scale disasters, which may be either natural disasters or disasters caused by humans (Suarez-Ojeda & Autler, 2003). 100 Resilient Cities (100RC) was founded in 2013 to support urban resilience which is "the capacity of individuals, communities, institutions, businesses, and systems within a city to survive, adapt, and grow no matter what kinds of chronic stresses and acute shocks they experience" (100 Resilient Cities [100RC], 2019). 100RC described resilient cities as reflective, resourceful, inclusive, integrated, robust, redundant, and flexible; many of these attributes align with a resilient, mindful, and reflective approach to leadership. 100RC acknowledges the role of both chronic stresses (unemployment, inadequate transportation, etc.) and acute shocks (natural disasters, terrorist attacks) as well as the interplay between the two (100RC, 2019). In one example, Hurricane Katrina was devastating for New Orleans, but the disaster was exacerbated by chronic stressors including poverty, racism, and inadequate infrastructure, among other challenges (100RC, 2019). An urban resilience framework acknowledges the myriad of complex challenges faced by cities and the interconnected nature of systems. Wheatley (2006) described a new way of approaching leadership that acknowledged the role of chaos: changes in one part of an interconnected system cascade and create chaos that reorganizes to a new form. This self-organizing and adaptation takes place through relationships and creativity, not control and order (Wheatley, 2006). In the face of chaos, resilience becomes less about having the perfect plan and more about shaping a built environment that is responsive while also developing relationships among the many individuals who will respond to the crisis.

Following the mass shooting at the Pulse nightclub in Orlando, nursing leaders reflected on the preparation that enabled them to respond to the situation and provide quality patient care (Willis & Philp, 2017). Orlando Regional Medical Center was prepared because they had planned, practiced, and debriefed simulations; developed a strong culture of teamwork through relationship building; and created a culture of resiliency and trust by involving frontline staff in decision-making (Willis & Philp, 2017). Reflection in leadership learning is critical for leaders to be able to take in, process, evaluate, and learn from experience while also responding to external stimuli and engaging with others. Managing change is also supported by mindfulness. In a study of senior staff members who facilitated strategic organizational change initiatives, Chesley and Wylson (2016) found change leaders who were more mindful were better able to manage the ambiguity. Rather than seeking to escape the ambiguity, or rush through the neutral zone (Bridges, 2016), they practiced self-awareness and engaged in self-care while also supporting team members by providing coaching and encouragement (Chesley & Wylson, 2016). Because of the mindful approach, which allowed them to see ambiguity as more neutral rather than threatening, they were also better able to engage in help seeking behaviors from executives, mentors, or coaches (Chesley & Wylson, 2016). Mindfulness is key for managing transitions and providing support for team members experiencing change and transition.

In examining the power of mindful, resilient, reflective leadership learning on a broader scale, we return to the study by Parks Daloz et al. (1996). Of the over 100 people they interviewed, all were committed to the common good and most demonstrated perseverance and resilience, having been in their roles for many years. All of the participants had ethical congruence in their life and work, which included engagement with diversity and complexity. In looking at the lives of commitment lived by the participants, and reflecting on the implications of the study, the authors established primary directions to orient the work of sectors such as education, business, healthcare, religion, and other areas of society that influence our collective well-being (Parks Daloz et al., 1996). Their implications resonate with the reflection in leadership learning framework. It is important to take time to pause, reflect, and assess. Although we may feel inclined to work faster in the face of challenge, Parks Daloz et al. (1996) noted, "Creating time for reflection, learning, and reorientation can be a significant act of citizenship" (p. 214). Stopping to ask questions and assess actions facilitates purpose when addressing complex challenges. We need to prioritize creating strong relationships, both in our communities and through sustained dialogue with others (Parks Daloz et al., 1996). The authors underscored the importance of dialogue: "it is significant that we found *constructive engagements with otherness* to be the single most critical element undergirding commitment to the common good" (Parks Daloz et al., 1996, p. 215, emphasis in original). Through practicing conscious connection, we move beyond individualism toward communities of mutual respect where we are empowered and enabled to ask broader questions about the common good (Parks Daloz et al., 1996). Finally, it is important to pay attention to language (Parks Daloz et al., 1996). Language is critically important for leadership (Guthrie & Jenkins, 2018) and it shapes who is included and who is excluded from conversations and experiences (Bertrand Jones et al., 2016). As learners are grounded in the reflection in leadership learning framework and supported by educators who are colearners, they are able to achieve personal and community outcomes that result in richly connected and purposeful lives.

REFLECTION IN LEADERSHIP LEARNING: PRESENCE AND THRIVING FOR THINKING AND CHANGE

Reflection in leadership learning is essential for the development of individuals and communities that can and will create positive change. We are at a point in time where the news is full of crises. As we write this, the United States government just temporarily resolved the longest partial government shutdown in history. Within the past year, there has been news coverage of natural disasters including volcano eruptions, hurricanes, and wildfires of unprecedented scale, regular mass shootings, acts of racism, anti-immigrant protests as countries embrace nationalism, and the list could go on. These are not challenges that can be resolved with technical fixes; these are concerns that require deep reflection, transformational thinking, and inclusive leadership. We need reflective, mindful, and resilient leaders working in community for the common good; the only way out is through, and the only way through is by developing and applying these important skills. The world is changing, and as quickly as we begin to manage one transition, we are met with another. This work requires experiential leadership learning and reflection that promote deep learning. It requires critical reflection that questions assumptions and leads to action for justice. It requires reflective leadership educators to hold space and engage in the self-work required to facilitate reflection for learners. As a mindful community, we can embrace presence to better understand our individual and shared reactions. As a resilient community, we can not only respond to changes but use adaptive skills to plan for the future. Reflective leadership learners initiate, facilitate, and make meaning of change and transition.

If we spend too much time thinking, we risk becoming immobilized by our thought processes; if we rush into uninformed action, we risk doing more harm than good. By finding the iterative ebb and flow between engaging in critical reflection, alone and with others, and taking action on our reflections in community, we engage in reflection in leadership learning. Reflection is essential for leaders to embrace complexity and engage in the leadership process in order to create more inclusive, just, and equitable communities.

REFERENCES

100 Resilient Cities. (2019). What is urban resilience?. Retrieved from http://100resilientcities.org/resources/

Association of American Colleges and Universities. (2009). Inquiry and analysis VALUE rubric. Retrieved from https://www.aacu.org/value/rubrics/critical-thinking

Association of American Colleges and Universities. (2009). Critical thinking VALUE rubric. Retrieved from https://www.aacu.org/value/rubrics/critical-thinking

Abbott, H. P. (2008). *The Cambridge introduction to narrative* (2nd ed.). Cambridge, England: Cambridge University Press.

Ahlquist, J. (2016). The digital identity of student affairs professionals. In E. T. Cabellon & J. Ahlquist (Eds.), *New Directions for Student Services: No. 155. Engaging the digital generation* (pp. 29–46). San Francisco, CA: Jossey-Bass.

Ahlquist, J. (2017). Digital student leadership development. In J. Ahlquist & L. Endersby (Eds.), *New Directions for Student Leadership: No. 153. Going digital in student leadership* (pp. 47–62). San Francisco, CA: Jossey-Bass.

Ahlquist, J., & Endersby, L. (2017). Editors notes. In J. Ahlquist & L. Endersby (Eds.), *New Directions for Student Leadership: No. 153. Going digital in student leadership* (pp.5–8). San Francisco, CA: Jossey-Bass.

Allen, S. J., Shankman, M. L., & Miguel, R. F. (2012). Emotionally intelligent leadership: An integrative, process oriented theory of student leadership. *Journal of Leadership Education, 11*(1), 177–203.

Allen, S. J., & Shehane, M. R. (2016). Exploring the language of leadership learning and education. In D. M. Roberts & K. J. Bailey (Eds.), *New Directions for Student Leadership: No. 151. Assessing student leadership* (pp. 35–49). San Francisco, CA: Jossey-Bass.

Alvarez, C. (2017). Controversy with civility. In S. R. Komives., W. Wagner., & Associates (Eds.), *Leadership for a better world: Understanding the social change model of leadership development* (pp.149– 170). San Francisco, CA: Jossey-Bass.

Thinking to Transform: Reflection in Leadership Learning
pp. 135–152
Copyright © 2019 by Information Age Publishing

Andenoro, A. C., Allen, S. J., Haber-Curran, P., Jenkins, D. M., Sowcik, M., Dugan, J. P., & Osteen, L. (2013). *National leadership education research agenda 2013–2018: Providing strategic direction for the field of leadership education.* Retrieved from http://leadershipeducators.org/ResearchAgenda

Anderson, L. W., & Krathwohl, D. R. (Eds.). (2001). *A taxonomy for learning, teaching, and assessing: A revision of Bloom's taxonomy of education objectives.* New York, NY: Pearson.

Angelo, T. A., & Cross, K. P. (1993). *Classroom assessment techniques: A handbook for teachers.* San Francisco, CA: Jossey-Bass.

Antonacopoulou, E. P., & Bento, R. F. (2004). Methods of 'learning leadership': Taught and experiential. *Leadership in organizations: Current issues and key trends,* 81–102.

Ash, S. L., & Clayton, P. H. (2004). The articulated learning: An approach to guided reflection and assessment. *Innovative Higher Education, 29*(2), 137–154.

Ash, S. L., & Clayton, P. H. (2009). Generating, deepening, and documenting learning: The power of critical reflection in applied learning. *Journal of Applied Learning in Higher Education, 1*(1), 25–48.

Ash, S. L., Clayton, P. H., & Atkinson, M. P. (2005). Integrating reflection and assessment to capture and improve student learning. *Michigan Journal of Community Service Learning,* 49–60.

Astin, A. W. (1984). Student Involvement: A developmental theory for higher education. *Journal of College Student Development, 40*(5), 518–529.

Astin, A. W., Astin, H. S., & Lindholm, J. A. (2011). *Cultivating the spirit: How college can enhance students' inner lives.* San Francisco, CA: John Wiley & Sons.

Astin, A. W., Vogelgesang, L. J., Ikeda, E. K., & Yee, J. A. (2000). *How service learning affects students.* Los Angeles, CA: Higher Education Research Institute.

Avolio, B. J., & Gardner, W. L. (2005). Authentic leadership development: Getting to the root of positive forms of leadership. *The Leadership Quarterly, 16*(3), 315–338.

Avolio, B. J., & Hannah, S. T. (2008). Developmental readiness: Accelerating leadership development. *Consulting Psychology Journal: Practice and Research, 60*(4), 331–347.

Ayman, R., Adams, S., Fisher, B., & Hartmen, E. (2003). Leadership development in higher education institutions: A present and future perspective. In S. E. Murphy & R. E. Riggio (Eds.), *The future of leadership development* (pp. 201–222). Mahwah, NJ: Erlbaum.

Bahns, A. J., Preacher, K. J., Crandall, C. S., & Gillath, O. (2016). Similarity in relationships as niche construction: Choice, stability, and influences within dyads in a free choice environment. *Journal of Personality and Social Psychology 112*(2), 329–355.

Bandura, A. (1977). *Social learning theory.* Englewood Cliffs, NJ: Prentice Hall.

Bandura, A. (1997). *Self-efficacy: The exercise of control.* New York, NY: W.H. Freeman.

Bandura, A. (1998). Personal and collective efficacy in human adaptation and change. In J. G. Adair, D. Belanger, & K. L. Dion (Eds.), *Advances in psycholog-*

ical science, personal, social and cultural aspects (1st ed., pp. 51–71). London, England: Psychology Press.

Barbezat, D. P., & Bush, M. (2014). *Contemplative practices in higher education: Powerful methods to transform teaching and learning.* San Francisco, CA: Jossey-Bass.

Barr, R. B., & Tagg, J. (1995). From teaching to learning—A new paradigm for undergraduate education. *Change: The Magazine of Higher Learning, 27*(6), 12–26.

Baruch, R., & Stutman, S. (2003). The yin and yang of resilience. In E. H. Grotberg (Ed.), *Resilience for today: Gaining strength from adversity* (pp. 31–52). Westport, CT: Praeger.

Bass, R. V., & Good, J. W. (2004). Educare and educere: Is a balance possible in the educational system. *The Educational Forum, 68,* 161–168.

Baumgartner, L. M. (2012). Mezirow's theory of transformative learning from 1975 to present. In E. W. Taylor, P. Cranton, & Associates (Eds.), *The handbook of transformative learning: Theory, research, and practice* (pp. 99–115). San Francisco, CA: John Wiley & Sons.

Bean, T. W., & Stevens, L. P. (2002). Scaffolding reflection for preservice and inservice teachers. *Reflective Practice, 3*(2), 205–218.

Beauchamp, C. (2015). Reflection in teacher education: Issues emerging from a review of current literature. *Reflective Practice, 16*(1), 123–141.

Belenky, M., Clinchy, B., Goldberger, N., & Trule, J. (1986). *Women's ways of knowing.* New York, NY: Basic Books.

Bertrand Jones, T., Guthrie, K. L., & Osteen, L. (2016). Critical domains of culturally relevant leadership learning: A call to transform leadership programs. In K. L. Guthrie, T. Bertrand Jones, & L. Osteen (Eds.), *New Directions for Student Leadership: No. 152. Developing culturally relevant leadership learning* (pp. 9–21). San Francisco, CA: Jossey-Bass.

Biddix, J. P. (2018). *Research methods and applications for student affairs.* San Francisco, CA: John Wiley & Sons.

Birkelund, R. (2000). Ethics and education. *Nursing Ethics, 7*(6), 473–480.

Bloom, B. S. (Ed.). (1956). *Taxonomy of educational objectives, handbook I: Cognitive domain.* New York, NY: David McKay.

Bohecker, L., Vereen, L. G., Wells, P. C., & Wathen, C. C. (2016). A mindfulness experiential small group to help students tolerate ambiguity. *Counselor Education & Supervision, 55,* 16–30.

Bonnet, J. (2017). Citizenship. In S. R. Komives, W. Wagner, & Associates (Eds.), *Leadership for a better world: Understanding the social change model of leadership development* (pp. 175–196). San Francisco, CA: Jossey-Bass.

Borton, T. (1970). *Reach, touch, and teach: Student concerns and process education.* New York, NY: McGraw-Hill.

Boud D., Keogh, R., & Walker, D. (1985a). Promoting reflection in learning: A model. In D. Boud, R. Keogh, & D. Walker (Eds.), *Reflection: Turning experience into learning* (pp. 18–40). New York, NY: RoutledgeFalmer.

Boud D., Keogh, R., & Walker, D. (1985b). What is reflection in learning? In D. Boud, R. Keogh, & D. Walker (Eds.), *Reflection: Turning experience into learning* (pp. 7–17). New York, NY: RoutledgeFalmer.

Boyd, B., & Williams, J. (2010) Developing life-long learners through personal growth projects. *Journal of Leadership Education, 9*(2), 144–150.

Bresciani, M. J., Gardner, M. M., & Hickmott, J. (2012). *Demonstrating student success, a practical guide to outcomes-based assessment of learning and development in student affairs.* Sterling, VA: Stylus.

Bridges, W. (2016). *Managing transitions: Making the most of change* (4th ed.). Boston, MA: Da Capo Press.

Brookfield, S. D. (2000). Transformative learning as ideology critique. In J. Mezirow & Associates (Eds.), *Learning as transformation: Critical perspectives on a theory in process* (pp. 125–148). San Francisco, CA: Jossey-Bass.

Brookfield, S. (2009). The concept of critical reflection: Promises and contradictions. *European Journal of Social Work, 12*(3), 293–304.

Brookfield, S. D. (2017). *Becoming a critically reflective teacher* (2nd ed). San Francisco, CA: Jossey-Bass.

Brungardt, C. L. (1996). The making of leaders: A review of the research in leadership development and education. *The Journal of Leadership Studies, 3*(3), 81–95.

Burchell, H., & Dyson, J. (2005). Action research in higher education: Exploring ways of creating and holding the space for reflection. *Educational Action Research, 13*(2), 291–300.

Burciaga, R., & Navarro, N. C. (2015). Educational testimonio: Critical pedagogy as mentorship. In C. S. Turner (Ed.), *New Directions for Higher Education: No. 171. Mentoring as transformative practice: Supporting student and faculty diversity* (pp. 33–41). San Francisco, CA: Jossey-Bass.

Burkhardt, J. C., & Zimmerman-Oster, K. (1999). How does the richest, most widely educated nation prepare leaders for its future? *Proteus, 16*(2), 9.

Burns, J. M. (1978). *Leadership.* New York, NY: Harper & Row.

Burton, A. J. (2000). Reflection: Nursing's practice and education panacea? *Journal of Advanced Nursing, 31*(5), 1009–1017.

Buschlen, E., & Guthrie, K. L. (2014). Seamless leadership learning in curricular and cocurricular facets of university life: A pragmatic approach to praxis. *Journal of Leadership Studies, 7*(4), 58–63.

Campbell, F. C. (Ed.). (2008). *Elements of metallurgy and engineering alloys.* Materials Park, OH: ASM International.

Campbell, C., & Baikie, G. (2013). Teaching critically reflective analysis in the context of a social justice course. *Reflective Practice, 14*(4), 452–464.

Center for Contemplative Mind in Society. (2014) The tree of contemplative practices. Retrieved from http://www.contemplativemind.org/practices/tree

Center for Contemplative Mind in Society. (2018). *Contemplative community in higher education: A toolkit.* Retrieved from http://www.contemplativemind.org/files/Toolkit021618web.pdf

Chaumba, J. (2015). Using blogs to stimulate reflective thinking in a human behavior course. *Social Work Education, 34*(4), 377–390.

Chesley, J., & Wylson, A. (2016). Ambiguity: The emerging impact of mindfulness for change leaders. *Journal of Change Management, 16*(4), 317–336.

Chirema, K. D. (2007). The use of reflective journals in the promotion of reflection and learning in post-registration nursing students. *Nurse Education Today,* 27, 192–202.

Christman, D. E., & McClellan, R. L. (2012). Discovering middle space: Distinctions of sex and gender in resilient leadership. *The Journal of Higher Education,* 83(5), 648–670.

Chu, S. K. W., Chan, C. K. K., & Tiwari, A. F. Y. (2012). Using blogs to support learning during internship. *Computers & Education, 58,* 989–1000.

Chunoo, V., & Osteen, L. (2016). Purpose, mission, and context: The call for educating future leaders. In K. L. Guthrie & L. Osteen (Eds.), *New Directions for Higher Education: No. 174. Reclaiming higher education's purpose in leadership development* (pp. 9–20). San Francisco, CA: Jossey-Bass.

Cilente Skendall, K. (2017). An overview of the social change model of leadership development. In S. R. Komives, W. Wagner, & Associates (Eds.), *Leadership for a better world: Understanding the social change model of leadership development* (pp. 17–40). San Francisco, CA: Jossey-Bass.

Collins, S. (2017). Social workers and resilience revisited. *Practice: Social Work in Action, 29*(2), 85–105.

Conger, J. (1992). *Learning to lead: The art of transforming managers into leaders.* San Francisco, CA: Jossey-Bass.

Conger, J. A. (2004). Developing leadership capability: What's inside the black box? *Academy of Management Executive, 18*(3), 136–139.

Cooper, J. E., & Stevens, D. D. (2006). Journal-keeping and academic work: Four cases of higher education professionals. *Reflective Practitioner, 7*(3), 349–366.

Correia, M. G., & Bleicher, R. E. (2008). Making connections to teach reflection. *Michigan Journal of Community Service Learning, 14*(2), 41–49.

Cotton, A. H. (2001). Private thoughts in public sphere: Issues in reflection and reflective practices in nursing. *Nursing Theory and Concept Development or Analysis, 36*(4), 512–519.

Coulson, D., & Harvey, M. (2013). Scaffolding student reflection for experience-based learning: A framework. *Teaching in Higher Education, 18*(4), 401–413.

Coutu, D. (2002). How resilience works. *Harvard Business Review, 80*(5), 46–55.

Coyle, S. (2011). *Sustainable and resilient communities: A comprehensive action plan for towns, cities, and regions.* Hoboken, NJ: John Wiley & Sons.

Cranton, P. (2002). Teaching for transformation. In J. M. Ross-Gordon (Ed.), *New Directions for Adult & Continuing Education: No. 93. Contemporary viewpoints on teaching adults effectively* (pp. 63–72). Hoboken, NJ: John Wiley & Sons.

Cranton, P. (2006). Fostering authentic relationships in the transformative classroom. In E. W. Taylor (Ed.), *New Directions for Adult & Continuing Education: No. 109. Teaching for change: Fostering transformative learning in the classroom* (pp. 5–13). Hoboken, NJ: John Wiley & Sons.

Cranton, P., & Taylor, E.W. (2012). Transformative learning theory: Seeking a more unified theory. In E. W. Taylor, P. Cranton, & Associates (Eds.), *The handbook of transformative learning: Theory, research, and practice* (pp. 3–20). San Francisco, CA: John Wiley & Sons.

d'Arlach, L., Sánchez, B., & Feuer, R. (2009). Voices from the community: A case for reciprocity in service learning. *Michigan Journal of Community Service Learning*, 5–16.

Daudelin, M. W. (1996). Learning from experience through reflection. *Organizational Dynamics, 24*(3), 36–48.

Davies, M. (2015). A model of critical thinking in higher education. In M. B. Paulsen (Ed.), *Higher education: Handbook of theory and research,* (pp. 41–92). Switzerland: Springer International.

Davies, M., & Barnett, R. (Eds.). (2015). Introduction. In *The Palgrave handbook of critical thinking in higher education.* (pp. 1–25). New York, NY: Routledge-Falmer.

Day, D. V. (2000). Leadership development: A review in context. *Leadership Quarterly, 11*(4), 581–613.

Day, D. V., Harrison, M. M., & Halpin, S. M. (2009). *An integrative theory of leadership development: Connecting adult development, identity, and expertise.* New York, NY: Psychology Press.

Densten, I. L., & Gray, J. H. (2001). Leadership development and reflection: What is the connection. *The International Journal of Educational Management, 15*(3), 119–124.

Denzine, G. (1999). Personal and collective efficacy: Essential components of college students' leadership development. *Concepts & Connections: A Newsletter for Leadership Educators from the National Clearinghouse for Leadership Programs, 8*(1), 1, 3–5.

DeRosier, M. E., Frank, E., Schwartz, V., & Leary, K. A. (2013). The potential role of resilience education for preventing mental health problems for college students. *Psychiatric Annals, 43*(12), 538–544.

Dewey, J. (1933). *How we think: A restatement of the relation of reflective thinking to the educative process.* Boston, MA: D.C. Heath and Company.

Duckworth, A. (2016). *Grit: The power of passion and perseverance.* New York, NY: Scribner.

Dugan, J. P. (2012). Exploring local to global leadership education assessment. In K. L. Guthrie & L. Osteen (Eds.), *New Directions for Student Services: No. 140. Developing students' leadership capacity* (pp. 89–101). San Francisco, CA: Jossey-Bass.

Dugan, J. P. (2017). *Leadership theory: Cultivating critical perspectives.* San Francisco, CA: Jossey-Bass.

Dugan, J. P., & Komives, S. R. (2007). *Developing leadership capacity in college students: Findings from a national study.* A Report from the Multi-Institutional Study of Leadership. College Park, MD: National Clearinghouse for Leadership Programs.

Dugan, J. P., & Komives, S. R. (2011). Leadership theories. In S. R. Komives, J. P., Dugan, J. E. Owen, C. Slack, W. Wagner, & Associates (Eds.), *The handbook of student leadership development* (2nd ed., pp. 35–58). San Francisco, CA: Jossey-Bass.

Dugan, J. P., Kodama, C., Correia, B., & Associates. (2013). *Multi-Institutional Study of Leadership insight report: Leadership program delivery.* College Park, MD: National Clearinghouse for Leadership Programs.

Dweck, C. S. (2006). *Mindset: The new psychology of success*. New York, NY: Random House.

Dweck, C. S. (2016). What having a "growth mindset" actually means. *Harvard Business Review, 13*, 2–4.

Dyment, J. E., & O'Connell, T. S. (2014). When the ink runs dry: Implications for theory and practice when educators stop keeping reflective journals. *Innovative Higher Education, 39*, 417–429.

Early, S., & Fincher, J.(2017). Consciousness of self. In S. R. Komives, W. Wagner, & Associates (Eds.), *Leadership for a better world: Understanding the social change model of leadership development* (pp. 43–65). San Francisco, CA: Jossey-Bass.

Eich, D. (2008). A grounded theory of high-quality leadership programs: Perspectives from student leadership programs in higher education. *Journal of Leadership & Organizational Studies, 15*(2), 176–187.

Eyler, J. (2001). Creating your reflection map. In M. Canada & B. W. Speck (Eds.), *New Directions for Higher Education: No. 114. Developing and implementing service-learning programs* (pp. 35–43). San Francisco, CA: Jossey-Bass.

Eyler, J., & Giles, D. E. (1999). *Where's the learning in service-learning?* San Francisco, CA: Jossey-Bass.

Eyler, J., Giles, D. E., & Schmeide, A. (1996). *A practitioner's guide to reflection in service learning: Student voices and reflections*. A Technical Assistance Project funded by the Corporation for National Service. Nashville, TN: Vanderbilt University.

Felten, P., Gilchrist, L. Z., & Darby, A. (2006). Emotion and learning: Feeling our way toward a new theory of reflection in service-learning. *Michigan Journal of Community Service Learning*, 38–46.

Ferguson, J. L., Makarem, S. C., & Jones, R. E. (2016). Using a class blog for student experiential learning reflection in business courses. *Journal of Education for Business, 91*(1), 1–10.

Fernsten, L., & Fernsten, J. (2005). Portfolio assessment and reflection: Enhancing learning through reflective practice. *Reflective Practice, 6*(2), 303–309.

Fink, L. D. (2013). *Creating significant learning experiences*. San Francisco, CA: John Wiley & Sons.

Flavell, J. H. (1976). Metacognitive aspects of problem solving. In L. B. Resnick (Ed.), *The nature of intelligence* (pp. 231–236). Hillsdale, NJ: Erlbaum.

Fogarty, R., & Pete, B. (2018). *Metacognition: The neglected skill set for empowering students*. Cheltenham, Victoria, Australia: Hawker Brownlow.

Folke, C. (2016). Resilience (Republished). *Ecology and Society, 21*(4).

Fook, J., & Gardner, F. (2007). *Practising critical reflection: A resource handbook*. Berkshire, England: Open University Press.

Fook, J. (2016). *Social work: A critical approach to practice* (3rd ed.). Thousand Oaks, CA: SAGE.

Frankl, V. E. (2006). *Man's search for meaning*. Boston, MA: Beacon Press. (Original work published 1946)

Freire, P. (1996). *Pedagogy of the oppressed*. London, England: Penguin. (Original work published 1970)

Fritz, M. R., & Guthrie, K. L. (2017). Values clarification: Essential for leadership learning. *Journal of Leadership Education, 16*(1), 47–63.

Frost, N. (2010). Professionalism and social change: The implications of social change for the 'reflective practitioner'. In H. Bradbury, N. Frost, S. Kilminster, & M. Zukas (Eds.), *Beyond reflective practice: New approaches to professional lifelong learning* (pp. 15–24). New York, NY: Routledge.

Furman, R., Coyne, A., & Negi, N. J. (2008). An international experience for social work students: Self-reflection through poetry and journal writing exercises. *Journal of Teaching in Social Work, 28*(1/2), 71–85.

Garrity, M. K. (2013). Developing nursing leadership skills through reflective journaling: A nursing professor's personal reflection. *Reflective Practice, 14*(1), 118–130.

Gazella, K. A. (2005). Jon Kabat-Zinn, PhD: Bringing mindfulness to medicine. *Alternative Therapies, 11*(3), 56–64.

Gifford, G. T. (2010). A modern technology in the leadership classroom: Using B logs for critical thinking development. *Journal of Leadership Education, 9*(1), 165–172.

Goleman, D. (1995). *Emotional intelligence.* New York, NY: Bantam Books.

Goleman, D. (1998). The emotional intelligence of leaders. *Leader to Leader, 10,* 20–26.

Gordon Brown, P. (2016). College student development in digital spaces. In E. T. Cabellon & J. Ahlquist (Eds.), *New Directions in Student Services: No. 155. Engaging the digital generation* (pp. 59–73). San Francisco, CA: Jossey-Bass.

Gould, N., & Taylor, I. (1996). *Reflective learning for social work.* New York, NY: Routledge.

Grotberg, E. H. (Ed.). (2003a). Introduction: Resilience for today. In *Resilience for today: Gaining strength from adversity* (pp. ix–xiii). Westport, CT: Praeger.

Grotberg, E. H. (Ed.). (2003b). What is resilience? How do you promote it? How do you use it? In *Resilience for today: Gaining strength from adversity* (pp. 1–30). Westport, CT: Praeger.

Guthrie, K. L., & Bertrand Jones, T. (2012). Teaching and learning: Using experiential learning and reflection for leadership education. In K. L. Guthrie & L. Osteen (Eds.), *New Directions for Student Services: No. 140. Developing students' leadership capacity* (pp. 53–64). San Francisco, CA: Jossey-Bass.

Guthrie, K. L., Bertrand Jones, T., Osteen, L., & Hu, S. (2013). Cultivating leader identity and capacity in students from diverse backgrounds. *ASHE Higher Education Report, 39,* 4.

Guthrie, K. L., & Osteen, L. (2016). Editor's notes. In. K. L. Guthrie & L. Osteen (Eds.), *New Directions for Higher Education: No. 174. Reclaiming higher education's purpose in leadership development* (pp. 5–8). San Francisco, CA: Jossey-Bass.

Guthrie, K. L., & Jenkins, D. M. (2018). *The role of leadership educators: Transforming learning.* Charlotte, NC: Information Age.

Guthrie, K. L., & Meriwether, J. L. (2018). Leadership development in digital spaces through mentoring, coaching, and advising. In L. J. Hastings & C. Kane (Eds.), *New Directions for Student Leadership: No. 158. Role of mentoring, coaching, and advising in developing leadership* (pp. 99–110). San Francisco, CA: Jossey-Bass.

Guthrie, K. L., & Thompson, S. (2010). Creating meaningful environments for leadership education. *Journal of Leadership Education, 9*(2), 50–57.

Haber-Curran, P., & Tillapaugh, D. (2013). Leadership learning through student-centered and inquiry-focused approaches to teaching adaptive leadership. *Journal of Leadership Education, 12*(1), 92–116.

Habermas, J. (1971). *Knowledge of human interests.* Boston, MA: Beacon.

Habermas, J. (1984). *The theory of communication action* (Vol. 2). Boston, MA: Beacon.

Halpern, D. F. (2014). *Thought and knowledge: An introduction to critical thinking* (5th ed., Vol. 2). New York, NY: Psychology Press.

Hamerlinck, J., & Plaut, J. (2014). *Asset-based community engagement in higher education.* Minneapolis, MN: Minnesota Campus Compact.

Hannigan, B. (2001). A discussion of the strengths and weaknesses of 'refection' in nursing practices and education. *Journal of Clinical Nursing, 10,* 278–283.

Harding, H. E. (2011). *"A place of becoming"—Leadership educators' experience teaching leadership: A phenomenological approach* (Doctoral dissertation). Retrieved from ProQuest Dissertations. (3449975).

Harper, S. R. (2011). Strategy and intentionality in practice. In J. H. Schuh, S. R. Jones & S. R. Harper (Eds.), *Student services: A handbook for the profession* (5th ed., pp. 287–302). San Francisco, CA: Jossey-Bass.

Harvey, M., & Jenkins, D. M. (2014). Knowledge, praxis, and reflection: The three critical elements of effective leadership studies programs. *Journal of Leadership Studies, 7,* 76–85.

Hatcher J. A., & Bringle, R. G. (1997). Reflection: Bridging the gap between service and learning. *College Teaching, 45*(4), 153–158.

Hattie, J., & Timperley, H. (2007). The power of feedback. *Review of Educational Research, 77*(1), 81–112.

Hatton, N., & Smith, D. (1995). Reflection in teacher education: Towards definition and implementation. *Teaching & Teacher Education, 11*(1), 33–49.

Heifetz, R. A. (1991). *Leadership without easy answers.* Cambridge, MA: Harvard Business Press.

Heifetz, R. A., & Linsky, M. (2002). *Leadership on the line: Staying alive during the dangers of leading.* Cambridge, MA: Harvard Business Press.

Higher Education Research Institute. (1996). *A social change model of leadership development: A guidebook.* Los Angeles, CA: The Regents of the University of California.

Hess, P. W. (2007). Enhancing leadership skill development by creating practice/feedback opportunities in the classroom. *Journal of Management Education, 31*(2), 195–213.

Hikida, M. (2018). Holding space for literate identity co-construction. *Journal of Literacy Research, 50*(2), 217–238.

Hill, E., Posey, T., Gómez, E., & Shapiro, S. L. (2018). Student readiness: Examining the impact of a university outdoor orientation program. *Journal of Outdoor Recreation, Education, and Leadership, 10*(2), 109–123.

Hirons, A. D. & Thomas, P. A. (2018). *Applied tree biology.* Hoboken, NJ: John Wiley & Sons.

hooks, b. (1994). *Teaching to transgress: Education as the practice of freedom*. New York, NY: Routledge.

Horton-Deutsch, S., & Sherwood, G. (2008). Reflection: An educational strategy to develop emotionally-competent nurse leaders. *Journal of Nursing Management, 16*, 946–954.

Houston, W. (1988). Reflecting on reflection In H. Waxman et al. (Eds.), *Images of reflection in teacher education* (pp. 2–9). Manassas, VA: ATE.

Howard, C. S., & Irving, J. A. (2014). The impact of obstacles defined by developmental antecedents on resilience in leadership formation. *Management Research Review, 37*(5), 466–478.

Hubbs, D., & Brand, C. F. (2010). Learning from the inside out: Methods for analyzing reflective journals in the college classroom. *Journal of Experiential Education, 33*(1), 56–71.

Huffaker, J. S., & West, E. (2005). Enhancing learning in the business classroom: An adventure with improve techniques. *Journal of Management Education, 29*(6), 852–869.

Hughes, R., Ginnett, R., & Curphy, G. (2012). *Leadership: Enhancing the lessons of experience*. New York, NY: McGraw-Hill.

Hunt, K. P., & Krakow, M. M. (2015). The best of both worlds: Exploring cross-collaborative community engagement. *The Journal of Effective Teaching, 15*(2), 87–98.

Hurtado, S., Milem, J., Clayton-Pedersen, A., & Allen, W. (1999). *Enacting diverse learning environments: Improving the climate for racial/ethnic diversity in higher education. ASHE Higher Education Report, 26:8*. John Wiley & Sons.

Jacoby, B. (2015). *Service-learning essentials: Questions, answers, and lessons learned*. San Francisco, CA: Jossey-Bass.

Johnson, J. (2009). Defining reflection in student affairs: A new culture of approach. *The Vermont Connection, 30*, 87–97.

Johnson, M. L., Taasoobshirazi, G., Kestler, J. L., & Cordova, J. R. (2015). Models and messengers of resilience: A theoretical model of college students' resilience, regulatory strategy use, and academic achievement. *Educational Psychology, 35*(7), 869–885.

Jones, S. R. (2016). Authenticity in leadership: Intersectionality of identities. In K. L. Guthrie, T. Bertrand Jones, & L. Osteen (Eds.), *New Directions for Student Leadership: No. 152. Developing culturally relevant leadership learning* (pp. 23–34). San Francisco, CA: Jossey-Bass.

Jones, S. R., & Abes, E. S. (2013). *Identity development of college students: Advancing frameworks for multiple dimensions of identity*. San Francisco, CA: John Wiley & Sons.

Kellerman, B. (2012). *The end of leadership*. New York, NY: HarperCollins.

Kember, D., McKay, J., Sinclair, K., & Wong Yuet, F. K. (2008). A four-category scheme for coding and assessing the level of reflection in written work. *Assessment & Evaluation in Higher Education, 33*(4), 369–379.

Kemmis, S. (1985). Action research and the politics of reflection. In D. Boud, R. Keogh, & D. Walker (Eds.), *Reflection: Turning experience into learning* (pp. 139–163). New York, NY: RoutledgeFalmer.

Kezar, A. J., Carducci, R., & Contreras-McGavin, M. (2006). Rethinking the "L" word in higher education. *ASHE Higher Education Report, 31:6*. Hoboken, NJ: Wiley and Sons.

Kilminster, S., Zukas, M., Bradbury, H., & Frost, N. (2010). Introduction and overview. In H. Bradbury, N. Frost, S. Kilminster, & M. Zukas (Eds.), *Beyond reflective practice: New approaches to professional lifelong learning* (pp. 1–10). New York, NY: Routledge.

Kitchenham, A. (2008). The evolution of John Mezirow's transformative learning theory. *Journal of Transformative Education, 6*(2), 104–123.

Kolb, D. A. (1984). *Experiential learning: Experience as the source of learning and development.* Upper Saddle River, NJ: Prentice-Hall.

Komives, S. R., Owen, J. E., Longerbeam, S. D., Mainella, F. C., & Osteen, L. (2005). Developing a leadership identity: A grounded theory. *Journal of College Student Development, 46*(6), 593–611.

Komives, S. R., Longerbeam, S. D., Owen, J. E., Mainella, F. C., & Osteen, L. (2006). A leadership identity development model: Applications from a grounded theory. *Journal of College Student Development, 47*(4), 401–418.

Komives, S. R., Lucas, N., & McMahon, T. R. (2013). *Exploring leadership: For college students who want to make a difference* (3rd ed.). San Francisco, CA: Jossey-Bass.

Komives, S. R., Wagner, W., & Associates. (2009). *Leadership for a better world: Understanding the Social Change Model of Leadership Development.* San Francisco, CA: Jossey-Bass.

Kostadin, K., Hunter, J. F., Proulx, J., Pressman, S. D., Dunn, E. (2019). Smartphones reduce smiles between strangers. *Computers in Human Behavior, 91*, 12–16.

Kotter, J. P. (2012). *Leading change.* Boston, MA: Harvard Business Review Press.

Kouzes, J. M., & Posner, B. Z. (2007). *The leadership challenge: The most trusted source on becoming a better leader.* San Francisco, CA: Jossey-Bass.

Krauss, S. E., & Hamid, J. A. (2015). Exploring the relationship between campus leadership development and undergraduate student motivation to lead among a Malaysian sample. *Journal of Further and Higher Education, 39*(1), 1–26.

Kreber, C. (2012). Critical reflection and transformative learning. In E. W. Taylor & P. Cranton (Eds.), *The handbook of transformative learning: Theory, research and practice* (pp. 323–340). San Francisco, CA: Jossey-Bass.

Kuhn, T. (1962). *The structure of scientific revolutions.* Chicago, IL: University of Chicago Press.

Ladson-Billings, G. (2014). Culturally relevant pedagogy 2.0: AKA the remix. *Harvard Educational Review, 84*(1), 74–84.

Larrivee, B. (2008). Meeting the challenge of preparing reflective practitioners. *The New Educator, 4*, 87–106.

Larsen, E. (1998). Feedback: Multiple purposes for management classrooms. *Journal of Management Education, 22*, 49–62.

Latina Feminist Group. (2001). *Telling to live: Latina feminist testimonios.* Durham, NC: Duke University Press.

Lau, J. Y. F. (2015). Metacognitive education: Going beyond critical thinking. In M. Davies, & R. Barnett (Eds.), *The Palgrave handbook of critical thinking in higher education.* (pp. 373–389). New York, NY: RoutledgeFalmer.

LeBlanc, R. G. (2017). Digital story telling in social justice nursing education. *Public Health Nursing, 34,* 395–400.

Le Cornu, A. (2009). Meaning, internalization, and externalization: Toward a fuller understanding of the process of reflection and its role in the construction of the self. *Adult Education Quarterly, 59*(4), 279–297.

Lewin, K. (1951). *Field theory in social sciences.* New York, NY: Harper & Row.

Lincoln, Y. S., & Guba, E. G. (2013). *The constructivist credo.* Walnut Creek, CA: Routledge.

Liu, K. (2015). Critical reflection as a framework for transformative learning in teacher education. *Educational Review, 67*(2), 135–157.

Lucas, N. (2015). Developing ethical leaders. In A. J. Schwartz (Ed.), *New Directions for Student Leadership: No. 146. When leading with integrity goes well: Integrating the mind, body, and heart* (pp. 61–69). San Francisco, CA: Jossey-Bass.

MacKeracher, D. (2012). The role of experience in transformative learning. In E. W. Taylor & P. Cranton (Eds.), *The handbook of transformative learning: Theory, research and practice* (pp. 342–354). San Francisco, CA: Jossey-Bass.

Maddux, H. C., & Donnett, D. (2015). John Dewey's pragmatism: Implications for reflection in service-learning. *Michigan Journal of Community Service Learning,* 64–73.

Mahatmya, D., Thurston, M., & Lynch, M. E. (2018). Developing students' well-being through integrative, experiential learning courses. *Journal of Student Affairs Research and Practice, 55*(3), 295–307.

Mahoney, A. D. (2017). Being at the heart of the matter: Culturally relevant leadership learning, emotions and storytelling. *Journal of Leadership Studies, 11*(3), 55–60.

Maloney, S., Tai, J. H. M., Lo, K., Molloy, E., & Ilic, D. (2013). Honesty in critically reflective essays: An analysis of student practice. *Advances in Health Sciences Education Theory Practice, 18,* 617–626.

Marzano, R. J. (2007). *The art and science of teaching: A comprehensive framework for effective instruction.* Alexandria, VA: ASCD.

Marzano, R. J., & Kendall, J. S. (2008). *Designing and assessing education objectives: Applying the new taxonomy.* Thousand Oaks, CA: Corwin Press.

Marzano, R. J., Pickering, D., & McTighe, J. (1993). *Assessing student outcomes: Performance assessment using the dimensions of the learning model.* Alexandria, VA: Association for Supervision and Curriculum Development.

Maslow, A. H. (1970). *Religions, values, and peak-experiences.* New York, NY: Penguin Books.

Mazza, N. (2003). *Poetry and therapy: Theory and practice.* New York, NY: Brunner-Routledge.

McNaughton, S. M. (2016). Critical reflection: Scaffolding social responsiveness for first-year students. *Reflective Practice, 17*(3), 296–307.

McPherson, J., & Mazza, N. (2014). Using arts activism and poetry to catalyze human rights engagement and reflection. *Social Work Education, 33*(7), 944–958.

Merriam, S. B. (2009). *Qualitative research: a guide to design and implementation*. San Francisco, CA: John Wiley & Sons.

Merriam, S. B., Caffarella, R.S., & Baumgartner. (2007). *Learning in adulthood: A comprehensive guide* (3rd ed.). San Francisco, CA: Jossey-Bass.

Mezirow, J. (1978a). *Education for perspective transformation: Women's re-entry programs in community colleges*. New York, NY: Teacher's College, Columbia University.

Mezirow, J. (1978b). Perspective transformation. *Adult Education, 28*, 1001–1110.

Mezirow, J. (1990). How critical reflection triggers transformative learning. In J. Mezirow & Associates (Eds.), *Fostering critical reflection in adulthood* (pp. 1–20). San Francisco, CA: Jossey-Bass.

Mezirow, J. (1991). *Transformative dimensions of adult learning*. San Francisco, CA: Jossey-Bass.

Mezirow, J. (Ed.). (2000). Learning to think like an adult: Core concepts of transformation theory. In *Learning as transformation: Critical perspectives on theory in progress* (pp. 3–33). San Francisco, CA: Jossey-Bass.

Mezirow, J. (2012). Learning to think like an adult: Core concepts of transformation theory. In E. W. Taylor & P. Cranton (Eds.), *The handbook of transformative learning: Theory, research and practice* (pp. 73–95). San Francisco, CA: Jossey-Bass.

Milem, J. F., Chang, M. J., & Antonio, A. L. (2005). *Making diversity work on campus: A research-based perspective*. Washington, DC: Association American Colleges and Universities.

Miller, S. (2005). What it's like being the 'holder of the space': A narrative on working with reflective practice in groups. *Reflective Practice: International and Multidisciplinary Perspectives, 6*(3), 367–377.

Miller-Young, J., Dean, Y., Rathburn, M., Petit, J. Underwood, M., Gleeson, J., … Clayton, P. (2015). Decoding ourselves: An inquiry into faculty learning about reciprocity in service-learning. *Michigan Journal of Community Service Learning*, 32–47.

Mitchell, T. D. (2008). Traditional vs. critical service-learning: Engaging the literature to differentiate two models. *Michigan Journal of Community Service Learning*, 50–65.

Mitchell, T. D., Donahue, D. M., & Young-Law, C. (2012). Service learning as a pedagogy of Whiteness. *Equity & Excellence in Education, 45*(4), 612–629.

Mitchell, T. D., Richard, F. D., Battastoni, R. M., Rost-Banik, C., Netz, R., & Zakoske, C. (2015). Reflective practice that persists: Connections between reflection in service-learning programs and in current life. *Michigan Journal of Community Service Learning*, 49–63.

Mitra, A. M. (2011). Learning how to look: The art of observation and leadership development. In M. Harvey & R. E. Riggio (Eds.). *Leadership studies: The dialogue of disciplines* (pp. 184–196). Northampton, MA: Edward Elgar.

Molee, L. M., Henry, M. E., Sessa, V. I., & McKinney-Prupis, E. R. (2010). Assessing learning in service-learning courses through critical reflection. *Journal of Experiential Education, 33*(3), 239–257.

Moon, J. A. (2004). *A handbook of reflective and experiential learning: Theory and practice*. London, England: RoutledgeFalmer.

Moon, J. A. (2006). *Learning journals: A handbook for reflective practice and professional development* (2nd ed.). New York, NY: Routledge.

Moon, J. A. (2010). *Using story: In higher education and professional development.* New York, NY: Routledge.

National Association of Colleges and Employers. (2019). *Career readiness defined.* Retrieved from http://www.naceweb.org/career-readiness/competencies/career-readiness-defined/

Nadler, L. (1984). *The handbook of human resource development.* San Francisco, CA: John Wiley & Sons.

Nandan, M., & London, M. (2013). Interdisciplinary professional education: Training college students for collaborative social change. *Education & Training, 55*(8/9), 815–835.

Newcomb, M., Burton, J., & Edwards, N. (2018). Pretending to be authentic: Challenges for students when reflective writing about their childhood for assessment. *Reflective Practice, 19*(3), 333–344.

Ng, P. T., & Tan, C. (2009). Community of practice for teachers: Sensemaking or critical reflective learning. *Reflective Practice, 10*(1), 37–44.

Northouse, P. (2016). *Leadership: Theory and practice* (7th ed.). Thousand Oaks, CA: SAGE.

Nugent, P., Moss, D., Barnes, R., & Wilks, J. (2011). Clear(ing) space: Mindfulness-based reflective practice. *Reflective Practice, 12*(1), 1–13.

O'Connell, T. S., & Dyment, J. E. (2011). The case of reflective journals: Is the jury still out? *Reflective Practice, 12*(1), 47–59.

Ostick, D. T., & Wall, V. A. (2011). Considerations for culture and social identity dimensions. In S. R. Komives, J. P. Dugan, J. E. Owen, C. Slack, & W. Wagner (Eds.), *The handbook for student leadership development* (2nd ed., pp. 339–368). San Francisco, CA: Jossey-Bass.

Overholt, J. R., & Ewert, A. (2015). Gender matters: Exploring the process of developing resilience through outdoor adventure. *Journal of Experiential Education, 38*(1), 41–55.

Owen, J. E. (2012). Using student development theories as conceptual frameworks in leadership education. In K. L. Guthrie & L. Osteen (Eds.), *New Directions for Student Services: No. 140. Developing students' leadership capacity* (pp. 17–35). San Francisco, CA: Jossey-Bass.

Owen, J. E. (2016). Fostering critical reflection: Moving from a service to a social justice paradigm. In W. Wagner & J. M. Pigza (Eds.), *New Directions for Student Leadership: No. 150. Leadership development through service-learning* (pp. 37–48). San Francisco, CA: Jossey-Bass.

Owen-Smith, P. (2018). *The contemplative mind in the scholarship of teaching and learning.* Bloomington, IN: Indiana University Press.

Palmer, P. J. (2017). *The courage to teach: Exploring the inner landscape of a teacher's life.* San Francisco, CA: John Wiley & Sons. (Original work published 1998)

Parks Daloz, L. A., Keen, C. H., Keen, J. P., & Daloz Parks, S. (1996). *Common fire: Leading lives of commitment in a complex world.* Boston, MA: Beacon Press.

Patton, L. D., Renn, K. A., Guido, F. M., Quaye, S. J. (2016). *Student development in college: Theory, research, and practice* (3rd ed.). San Francisco, CA: John Wiley & Sons.

Pew Research Center. (2018a). *Activism in the social media age.* Retrieved from http://www.pewinternet.org/2018/07/11/activism-in-the-social-media-age/

Pew Research Center. (2018b). *Teens, social media, & technology 2018.* Retrieved from http://www.pewinternet.org/2018/03/01/social-media-use-in-2018/

Piaget, J. (1970). *Genetic epistemology.* New York, NY: Columbia University Press.

Pigza, J. M. (2015). Navigating leadership complexity through critical, creative, and practical thinking. In S. R. Komives & K. L. Guthrie (Eds.), *New Directions for Student Leadership: No. 145. Innovative learning for leadership development* (pp. 35–48). San Francisco, CA: Jossey-Bass.

Postman, N., & Weingartner, C. (1969). *Teaching as a subversive activity.* New York, NY: Dell.

Preston, M., & Peck, A. (2016). Carts before horses? Remembering the primacy of the student's experience in student learning. In D. M. Roberts & K. J. Bailey (Eds.), *New Directions for Student Leadership: No. 151. Assessing Student Leadership* (pp. 79–91). San Francisco, CA: Jossey-Bass.

Price, D. M., Strodtman, L., Brough, E., Lonn, S., & Luo, A. (2015). Digital storytelling: An innovative technological approach to nursing education. *Nurse Educator, 40*(2), 66–70.

Przybylski, A. K., & Weinstein, N. (2012). Can you connect with me now? How the presence of mobile communication technology influence face-to-face conversation quality. *Journal of Social and Personal Relationships, 30*(3), 237–246.

Quinn, R. E. (1996). *Deep change: Discovering the leader within.* San Francisco, CA: Jossey-Bass.

Quinton, S., & Smallbone, T. (2010). Feeding forward: Using feedback to promote student reflection and learning—a teaching model. *Innovation in Education and Teaching International, 47* (1), 125–135.

Ramasubramanian, S. (2017). Mindfulness, stress coping and everyday resilience among emerging youth in a university setting: A mixed methods approach. *International Journal of Adolescence and Youth, 22*(3), 308–321.

Rendón, L. I. (2009). *Sentipensante pedagogy: Educating for wholeness, social justice, and liberation.* Sterling, VA: Stylus.

Reyes, K. B., & Curry Rodríguez, J. E. (2012). Testimonio: Origins, terms, and resources. *Equity & Excellence in Education, 45*(3), 525–538.

Rhodes, T. (2010). *Assessing outcomes and improving achievement: Tips and tools for using rubrics.* Washington, DC: Association of American Colleges and Universities.

Richardson, G. E. (2002), The metatheory of resilience and resiliency. *Journal of Clinical Psychology, 58,* 307–321.

Rievich, K., & Shatté, A. (2002). *The resilience factor: 7 keys to finding your inner strength and overcoming life's hurdles.* New York, NY: Broadway Books.

Roberts, D., & Ullom, C. (1989). Student leadership program model. *NASPA Journal, 27*(1), 67–74.

Roberts, D. C. (2007). *Deeper learning in leadership: Helping college students find the potential within.* San Francisco, CA: John Wiley & Sons.

Rodgers, C. (2002). Defining reflection: Another look at John Dewey and reflective thinking. *Teachers College Record, 104*(4), 842–866.

Rogers, R. R. (2001). Reflection in higher education: A concept analysis. *Innovative Higher Education, 26*(1), 37–57.

Rolf, J. E., & Glantz, M. D. (2002). Resilience: An interview with Norman Garmezy. In M. D. Glantz & J. L. Johnson (Eds.), *Resilience and development: Positive life adaptations* (pp. 5–16). New York, NY: Kluwer Academic.

Rolfe, G., Freshwater, D., & Jasper, M. (2001). *Critical reflection for nursing and the helping professions: A user's guide.* Basingstoke, England: Palgrave Macmillan.

Rosch, D. M., & Anthony, M. D. (2012). Leadership pedagogy: Putting theory to practice. In K. L. Guthrie & L. Osteen (Eds.), *New Directions for Student Services: No. 140. Developing student's leadership capacity* (pp. 53–64). San Francisco, CA: Jossey-Bass.

Rost, J. C. (1993). *Leadership for the twenty-first century.* New York, NY: Praeger.

Saldaña, J. (2013). *The coding manual for qualitative researchers* (3rd ed.). Thousand Oaks, CA: SAGE.

Sanford, N. (1967). *Where colleges fail: A study of the student as a person.* San Francisco, CA: Jossey-Bass.

Savicki, V., & Price, M. V. (2017). Components of reflection: A longitudinal analysis of study abroad student blog posts. *Frontiers: The Interdisciplinary Journal of Study Abroad, 29*(2), 51–62.

Scanlan, J. M., & Chernomas, W. M. (1997). Developing the reflective teacher. *Journal of Advanced Nursing, 25,* 1138–1143.

Schön, D. A. (1983). *The reflective practitioner: How professionals think in action.* New York, NY: Basic Books.

Seemiller, C., & Priest, K.L. (2015). The hidden "Who" in leadership education: Conceptualizing leadership educator professional identity development. *Journal of Leadership Education, 14*(3), 132–151.

Seemiller, C., Priest, K. L. (2017). Leadership educator journeys: Expanding a model of leadership educator professional identity development. *Journal of Leadership Education, 16*(2), 1–22.

Shankman, M. L., Allen, S. J., & Haber-Curran, P. (2015). *Emotionally intelligent leadership for students: Facilitation and activity guide* (2nd ed.). San Francisco, CA: Jossey-Bass.

Siebert, A. (2005). *The resiliency advantage: Master change, thrive under pressure, and bounce back from setbacks.* San Francisco, CA: Berrett-Koehler.

Silver, N. (2013). Reflective pedagogies and the metacognitive turn in college teaching. In M. Kaplan, N. Silver, D. LaVaque-Manty, & D. Meizlish (Eds.), *Using reflection and metacognition to improve student learning: Across the disciplines, across the academy* (pp. 1–17). Sterling, VA: Stylus.

Smalley, S. L., & Winston, D. (2010). *Fully present: The science, art, and practice of mindfulness.* Philadelphia, PA: Da Capo Press.

Sowcik, M., & Allen, S. J. (2013). Getting down to business: a look at leadership education in business schools. *Journal of Leadership Education, 12*(3), 57–75.

Speare, J., & Henshall, A. (2014). 'Did anyone think the trees were students?' Using poetry as a tool for critical reflection. *Reflective Practice, 15*(6), 807–820.

Stevens, D. D., & Cooper, J. E. (2009). *Journal keeping: How to use reflective writing for effective learning, teaching, professional insight, and positive change.* Sterling, VA: Stylus.

Stoller, E. (2013). Our shared future: Social media, leadership, vulnerability, and digital identity. *Journal of College and Character, 14* (1), 5–10.

Stone, D., & Heen, S. (2014). *Thanks for the feedback: The science and art of receiving feedback well.* New York, NY: Penguin Books.

Stuhr, P. T., Lecomte, H., & Sutherland, S. (2017). A portrait of social and emotional learning within Sequoia National Park. *Journal of Outdoor Recreation, Education, and Leadership, 9*(4), 403–424.

Sturgill, A., & Motley, P. (2014). Methods of reflection about service learning: Guided vs. free, dialogic vs. expressive, and public vs. private. *Teaching and Learning Inquiry, 2*(1), 81–93.

Suarez-Ojeda, E. N., & Autler, L. (2003). Community resilience: A social approach. In E. H. Grotberg (Ed.), *Resilience for today: Gaining strength from adversity* (pp. 189–210). Westport, CT: Praeger.

Sumka, S., Porter, M. C., & Piacitelli, J. (2015). *Working side by side: Creating alternative breaks as catalysts for global learning, student leadership, and social change.* Sterling, VA: Stylus.

Suskie, L. (2018). *Assessing student learning: A common sense guide* (3rd ed.). San Francisco, CA: John Wiley & Sons.

Taylor, E. W. (2009). Fostering transformative learning. In J. Mezirow & E. W. Taylor (Eds.), *Transformative learning in practice: Insights from community, workplace, and higher education* (pp. 3–17). San Francisco, CA: Jossey-Bass.

Taylor, B. J., Freshwater, D., Sherwood, G., & Esterhuizen, P. (2008). International perspectives in reflective practice: Global knowledge reservoirs. In D. Freshwater, B. Taylor, & G. Sherwood (Eds.), *International textbook of reflective practice in nursing* (pp. 71–96). Oxford, England: Blackwell.

Teig, T. (2018). *Higher education/student affairs master's students' preparation and development as leadership educators* (Doctoral dissertation). Retrieved from ProQuest Dissertations. (10826405).

Thompson, N., & Pascal, J. (2012). Developing critically reflective practice. *Reflective Practice, 13*(2), 311–325.

Thompson, S., & Thompson, N. (2008). *The critically reflective practitioner.* New York, NY: Palgrave Macmillan.

Thorpe, K. (2004). Reflective learning journals: From concept to practice. *Reflective Practice: International and Multidisciplinary Perspectives, 5*(3), 327–343.

Trowler, V. (2013). Leadership practices for student engagement in challenging conditions. *Perspectives: Policy and Practice in Higher Education, 17*(3), 91.

Turkle, S. (2015). *Reclaiming conversation: The power of talk in a digital age.* New York, NY: Penguin Books.

Wagner, W. (2017). Change. In S. R. Komives, W. Wagner, & Associates (Eds.), *Leadership for a better world: Understanding the social change model of leadership development* (pp. 201–232). San Francisco, CA: Jossey-Bass.

Wagner, W., & Pigza, J. M. (2016). The intersectionality of leadership and service-learning: A 21st-century perspective. In W. Wagner & J.M. Pigza (Eds.), *New Directions for Student Leadership, 150. Leadership development through service-learning* (pp. 11–22). San Francisco, CA: Jossey-Bass.

Walmsley, C., & Birkbeck, J. (2006). Personal narrative writing: A method of values reflection for BSW students. *Journal of Teaching in Social Work, 26*(1/2), 111–126.

Walumbwa, F. O., Avolio, B. J., Gardner, W. L., Wernsing, T. S., & Peterson, S. J. (2008). *Journal of Management, 34*(1), 89–126.

Ward, J. (2018) Lessons in resistance and resilience. *Diversity & Democracy: Civic Learning for Shared Futures, 21*(1).

Ward, J. R., & McCotter, S. S. (2004). Reflection as a visible outcome for preservice teachers. *Teaching and Teacher Education, 20*, 243–257.

Webster-Wright, A. (2013). The eye of the storm: A mindful inquiry into reflective practices in higher education. *Reflective Practice, 14*(4), 556–567.

Weick, K. E. (1995). *Sensemaking in organizations.* Thousand Oaks, CA: SAGE.

Weick, K. E., Sutcliffe, K. M., & Obstfeld, D. (2005). Organizing and the process of sensemaking. *Organization Science, 16*(4), 409–421.

Welch, M. (1999). The ABCs of reflection: A template for students and instructors to implement written reflection in service-learning. *NSEE Quarterly, 25*, 22–25.

Wheatley, M. J. (2006). *Leadership and the new science: Discovering order in a chaotic world* (3rd ed.). San Francisco, CA: Berrett-Koehler.

White, J. V. (2012). Students' perception of the role of reflection in leadership learning. *Journal of Leadership Education, 11*(2), 140–157.

White, J. V. (2014). *Students' application of leadership learning through reflection* (Doctoral dissertation). Retrieved from ProQuest Dissertations. (3625996).

White, J. V., & Guthrie, K. L. (2016). Creating a meaningful learning environment: Reflection in leadership education. *Journal of Leadership Education, 15*(1), 60–75.

White, S., Fook, J., & Gardner, F. (Eds.). (2006). *Critical reflection in health and social care.* New York, NY: Open University Press.

Willis, J., & Philp, L. (2017). Orlando Health nurse leaders reflect on the Pulse tragedy. *Nurse Leader, 15*(5), 319–322.

Wohlleben, P. (2015). *The hidden life of trees: What they feel, how they communicate discoveries from a secret world.* Vancouver, British Columbia, Canada: Greystone Books.

Wolf Williams, J. & Allen, S. (2015). Trauma-inspired prosocial leadership development. *Journal of Leadership Education, 14*(3), 86–103.

Yosso, T. J. (2005). Whose culture has capital? A critical race theory discussion of community cultural wealth. *Race Ethnicity and Education, 8*(1), 69–91.

Zimmerman-Oster, K., & Burkhardt, J. C. (1999). Leadership in the making: A comprehensive examination of the impact of leadership development programs on students. *The Journal of Leadership Studies, 6*(3/4), 50–66.

ABOUT THE AUTHORS

Dr. Jillian M. Volpe White serves as director of strategic planning and assessment in the Office of the Vice President for Student Affairs at Florida State University. She also serves as an affiliate instructor in the Department of Educational Leadership and Policy Studies and has taught in the Undergraduate Certificate in Leadership Studies. Jillian has more than 10 years of experience in community engagement and leadership development at the Florida State University Center for Leadership and Social Change and Florida Campus Compact. Through her work, she has served in roles that span the full range of experiential learning: as a service-learning student, nonprofit volunteer coordinator, service-learning instructor, community engagement coordinator, and experiential learning consultant. She received her doctorate of philosophy degree in higher education, master's degree in higher education, and undergraduate degree in mass media studies from Florida State University. Her research interests include reflection, experiential learning, leadership development, and student affairs assessment.

Dr. Kathy L. Guthrie is an associate professor of higher education in the Department of Educational Leadership and Policy Studies at Florida State University. In addition to teaching in the higher education program, Kathy also serves as director of the Leadership Learning Research Center, which coordinates the Undergraduate Certificate in Leadership Studies, and director of the Hardee Center for Leadership and Ethics in Higher Education. Her research focuses on the learning outcomes and environment of leadership and civic education, online teaching and learning, and professional development for student affairs professionals. Prior to becoming a faculty member, Kathy served as a student affairs administrator for 10 years in various functional areas including campus activities, commuter services, community engagement, and leadership development. She has worked in higher education administrative and faculty roles for more than 20 years and loves every minute of her chosen career path.

Dr. Maritza Torres is the assistant director for LEAD Scholars Academy at the University of Central Florida. Born and raised in Chicago, she received her bachelor's degree in communication with minors in Spanish and Latino studies from DePaul University and her master's degree in student personnel in higher education from the University of Florida. She received her PhD in higher education from Florida State University. At Florida State University, Dr. Torres was a graduate assistant for the Leadership Learning Research Center. Maritza's dissertation was centered on testimonios of Latina undergraduate women and their leader identity development in leadership courses and student organizations. Maritza previously worked at the University of Illinois Urbana-Champaign as a program advisor for the Illini Union Board and the University of Miami where she served as the assistant director of student activities and student organizations. Her research interests include: Latinx leadership, identity-based leadership, and culturally relevant leadership learning.